T0304973

MUSLIMS
DON'T
MATTER

Also by Sayeeda Warsi

The Enemy Within:
A Tale of Muslim Britain

MUSLIMS DON'T MATTER

SAYEEDA WARSI

**The
Bridge
Street
Press**

THE BRIDGE STREET PRESS

First published in Great Britain in 2024 by The Bridge Street Press

1 3 5 7 9 10 8 6 4 2

A CIP catalogue record for this book
is available from the British Library.

ISBN 978-0-349-13647-9

Typeset in Bembo by M Rules
Printed and bound in Great Britain by
Clays Ltd, Elcograf S.p.A.

Papers used by The Bridge Street Press are from well-managed forests
and other responsible sources.

The Bridge Street Press
An imprint of
Little, Brown Book Group
Carmelite House
50 Victoria Embankment
London EC4Y 0DZ

An Hachette UK Company
www.hachette.co.uk

www.littlebrown.co.uk

To the everyday decent folk of this great nation
who reject violence, division and hate.

To the stigmatised, stereotyped and silenced –
I hope this gives you a voice.

Contents

1

Buying Diamonds

So, I'm done with apologising.

I'm done with caveating my views, I'm done with condemning before I give myself the licence to speak. I'm done with feeling obliged to distance myself from the bad views of the bad Muslims. I'm done with being held accountable for the actions of any one of the almost two billion people in the world who follow the faith I was born into. I am done with having to explain and contextualise every word of a seventh-century religious book. I am done with appeasement, hoping that the climate would improve, that some in the media and politics will eventually tire of feeding the beast of division.

I'm done with fighting on terms set by the bigot and the Islamophobe – those that tie you up endlessly in peripheral arguments and accuse you of whataboutery when you try to calmly explain something in a context that suits their ultimately racist dispositions.

I'm done ingratiating myself with my fellow countrymen and women who seem to think that the darker your skin, the more damn grateful you should be for living in your own country. I'm done with explaining, justifying, defending, being held to a standard that others are not, and I'm done playing by the rules set by the racist.

Now I am past the age of fifty, I have both a sense of urgency and a new freedom. Time seems more precious and the climate more hostile than ever before. I'm done with being the acceptable, palatable Muslim.

Instead, I need to tell you bluntly exactly how I, and so many of my fellow British Muslims, feel right now.

We feel unwelcome and targeted. Awful rhetoric from politicians like Boris Johnson calling Muslim women 'bank robbers' and headlines like 'The Muslim problem' make us feel othered in our own country. Stripping citizenship from Muslims born and only ever having lived in the UK makes us feel like second-class Britons. We are shut out of decision-making through a policy of disengagement with Muslim organisations, pursued by both Labour and the Tories, that is now entering its seventeenth year. We feel mistrusted and misrepresented, stereotyped and stigmatised – the hundreds of corrections, apologies and successful libel cases against mainstream media outlets seem not to abate the thirst to demonise us. We feel isolated and yet stand accused of separatism. We are desperate to play our part in democracy, but when we do, we face accusations of entryism and takeovers.

We continue to have our loyalty questioned, however much we serve our nation. We died in the line of duty as doctors and nurses during Covid, as police officers and in the armed forces, yet we are still seen as the enemy. We are scrutinised and held to standards no other community is expected to meet, we are blamed for atrocities we have no connection to, we are held collectively accountable, and as far-right extremism has continued to rise and the government has over the years failed to focus on it, we feel unprotected and scared.

We feel like Muslims Don't Matter.

Recently, overt and unashamed Islamophobia has felt overwhelming.

In just the last twelve months, we've seen the ex-Home Secretary Suella Braverman write for *The Times* accusing peaceful protests about Israel's war in Gaza of being 'hate marches' and claiming 'Islamists, extremists and antisemites are in charge now'. In February 2024, the former deputy chairman of the Conservative Party, Lee Anderson, claimed London's Muslim mayor Sadiq Khan was controlled by 'Islamists'. ITV's political editor Robert Peston pointed out that if the word 'Islamist' had been replaced by 'Zionist' then there would have been no hesitation from the prime minister Rishi Sunak in condemning his MP's statements as antisemitic. Braverman was eventually sacked, and Anderson had the whip removed, yet Sunak could not bring himself to call their words Islamophobic. Why? Whether it was evidence of the desperate last gasps of a Conservative government that had run out of ideas and was using the culture war as a useful political tool, or because there's something specific about Muslims that doesn't elicit sympathy when they're victims of prejudice, it appears that for those in power Muslims Don't Matter.

In July 2024, Nigel Farage's Reform UK polled over 14 per cent, winning five seats.

Listening to the soft-ball interviews of their candidates by journalists and broadcasters during the campaign was galling. Racist tropes and stereotypes about Muslim 'breeding rates' – they're 'outnumbering' us, 'we are going to be in the minority' and 'they are going to take over' – imposing 'Sharia law' and not 'speaking English' were regularly made without robust challenge, along with even more sinister statements about Muslims being 'jihadis' who are 'wanting to kill us' and are our 'enemies'.

No other community would be spoken about in this way by individuals standing to be Members of Parliament. But for some in the media, Muslims are fair game. The climate has been perfectly poisoned to target British Muslims; to many of us, the far-right racist riots of summer 2024 had been many years in the making. Violence against Muslims started in Southport and swept across the country; Muslim pogroms manifested on our streets.

This violence follows years of demonising from some in government and the media, and comes in a wider context of fear and hate. According to Home Office statistics, in 2022/3, around 44 per cent of religiously motivated hate crime was directed at Muslims. Over the last few years, Muslims have consistently been the most targeted religious group. In June 2022, a survey of a number of mosques and

Islamic institutions found that 42 per cent had experienced religiously motivated attacks over the previous three years. Make no mistake, these are real threats.

In November 2023, a far-right teenager named Joe Metcalfe from Haworth, the quaint village once home to the Brontë sisters, was convicted of planning a terror attack on a mosque in Keighley, West Yorkshire. Metcalfe had 'made a detailed plan to murder Muslims at a nearby mosque while disguised as an armed police officer, record the killings and escape'.

Metcalfe 'idolised' Brenton Tarrant, the Australian white supremacist who murdered fifty-one worshippers at Friday congregational prayers at two mosques in Christchurch, New Zealand in 2019.

In 2021 Dean Morrice, an ex-UKIP member and former army driver, was jailed for eighteen years for possession of bomb-making materials. He presented himself as a caring family man and described himself as a patriot and a fan of Nigel Farage. He also revered Tarrant and had made a video of himself with a guitar, strumming along to the gunshots that rang out in the Christchurch terror attack.

Early in 2024, three men appeared at the Old Bailey accused of a far-right terror plot in which they allegedly used a 3D printer to produce a semi-automatic firearm. An Islamic centre in Leeds is said to have been one of their targets. One of the accused is from my home city of Wakefield. (They had not, at the time of writing, entered a plea but they currently enjoy the presumption of innocence and are due to be tried in March 2025.)

Conversations in Muslim homes up and down the country have increasingly become about this hostile climate and their future in the UK. We are scared. We are unsure about our future in our country. Many have made plans to move to other places in the world that they can call home. Many have discussed Plan Bs, and some have started to implement them.

My husband and I have had the conversation too. On one of our regular Sunday walks in Yorkshire, we sat in the courtyard at Nostell Priory for a coffee break. A conversation that started with mere concern took a darker turn as we started to plan investing in 'alternative assets' in the event of having to leave the UK, and leave quickly. We recalled how in the 1930s European Jews sewed precious stones into the seams of their jackets. Was it time for us to buy diamonds and keep a suitcase packed?

Growing up in the 1970s and 1980s in Dewsbury, West Yorkshire, my sisters and I would overhear our parents having hushed conversations about plans for when 'they throw us out'. In later life, we would become part of these conversations, which normally ended with us arguing with our parents and accusing them of being unnecessarily dramatic. Britain was home and had been for our family since the 1950s, when our grandfather arrived. How could anywhere else possibly be home? My parents ignored our protests and did invest in Pakistan, buying a sanctuary house of last resort in the country that their own parents had made their home after the partition of British India at the end of colonial rule in 1947. Since then, three of my four sisters have relented and made the same investment. But I continue to resist.

I refuse to accept that the country both my paternal and maternal grandfathers fought for during the Second World War in Aden and in Burma, a country for whom my great uncle was captured as a prisoner of war in Singapore, a country that one of my children serves in uniform, a country for which my family have a long and proud tradition of protecting is no longer safe for us. I am not prepared to leave a country my family have helped build. Instead of leaving my home, I have chosen to fight for my rightful place in it.

Before we carry on, let me explain exactly what I mean by Islamophobia.

Islamophobia or anti-Muslim racism should not be a new concept. As a country we have over the centuries often found ourselves directing hate and prejudice against those who live with us. Jews have been targeted in these islands since at least the twelfth century, when in 1190 an antisemitic pogrom in York led to the murder of 150 men, women and children in Clifford's Tower; homophobia in the twentieth century led the state to chemically castrate gay men, including the mathematician, Alan Turing; and anti-black racism led to the brutal killing of Stephen Lawrence on the streets of London in 1993. Islamophobia is simply the latest in a long line of prejudices that Britain is having to come to terms with, define and tackle.

Historically, British governments have not admitted to being sexist when they clearly were – when women were denied the vote, for example – or when they clearly were homophobic, as when a Conservative government under Margaret Thatcher introduced Section 28, or racist when they clearly were shown to be by the immigration rules that led to the Windrush scandal. Just as in previous times those in power were reluctant to acknowledge or challenge bigotry, we should not be surprised that the state once again refuses to acknowledge or challenge this latest form of bigotry.

Each time the bigots justified their prejudices, even rooted them in intellectual arguments suggesting women were inferior, gay men were unnatural and black communities were violent. Battles for equality had to be fought then and they are being fought again now. It seems we never learn from the mistakes of the past.

In 2017 a cross-party group of parliamentarians established an inquiry into Islamophobia which, over a year, held public meetings across the country, took oral evidence in Parliament and received hundreds of written submissions. They heard from a wide range of experts as well as victims and the communities impacted. They concluded that 'Islamophobia is rooted in racism and is a type of racism that targets expressions of Muslimness or perceived Muslimness'. In other words, it's anti-Muslim racism. This definition is not theologically based: it protects people, not religion. It has no interest in whether you are a practising Muslim or even a Muslim at all. As the report found, you can be targeted just for being 'perceived' to be Muslim.

This definition is criticised by some who argue that

Muslims are not a single race and thus don't deserve the protections we offer racial minorities. But their argument has no awareness that the racialisation of a group has nothing to do with their skin pigment.

This can be seen from long-running and well-documented academic work on racialisation. No one would argue that because Jews come in many shades – indeed as many as Muslims: black, brown, white and others – that they cannot be a race, and that they do not face racial discrimination because of their Jewishness.

Just as stereotypes about all Jews being rich and powerful are examples of anti-Jewish racism, so the stereotyping of all Muslims as uniquely violent, or anti-feminist or paedophiles is anti-Muslim racism.

Some argue that the discrimination cannot be racism because it's directed at religious belief. But again, we have precedent for this.

Religion or perceived religiousness as a factor in prejudice is not new. Antisemitism is often rooted in religious prejudice, for example when individuals are attacked for wearing Orthodox Jewish clothing or when synagogues and Jewish cemeteries are targeted. These attacks target Jewishness.

One of the examples in the Parliamentary report on Islamophobia came from a Sheffield mother, who gave evidence of her daughter being beaten up by her schoolfriends because she had started wearing a hijab. The attack resulted in the daughter suffering from depression and refusing to return to school. Wearing a headscarf made the girl a target. She was attacked for expressing her Muslimness.

Perhaps the most powerful examples are of those victims who face anti-Muslim racism but who are not in fact Muslim, only perceived to be so. In 2018, Ravneet Singh, a turban-wearing Sikh environmentalist, was attacked outside the Houses of Parliament on his way to visit an MP. The attacker grabbed at his turban and shouted, 'Muslim go back home.'

In 2015, far-right terrorist Zack Davies was convicted of the gruesome attempted murder of a Sikh dentist, Dr Sarandev Singh Bhambra. Attacking him in a Tesco in Mold, Wales with a hammer and machete, Davies assumed Dr Bhambra was Muslim due to the way he looked and claimed he 'did it for Lee Rigby', referring to the off-duty soldier killed in 2013 by two violent 'Islamists'. (Davies also claimed to be inspired by ISIS killer Jihadi John: violent extremists often have more in common with each other than the people they claim to represent.)

Neither Singh nor Bhambra were Muslim, but both were subjected to Islamophobic attacks.

Some claim that legitimate criticism of Islam could be chilled by claims of Islamophobia. The comedian Rowan Atkinson expressed his fear that religious hatred legislation will smuggle in a blasphemy law and stop people from mocking religion. (Atkinson has also said that Boris Johnson's description of Muslim women wearing face veils as 'letterboxes' was a 'pretty good' joke for which no apology was needed.)

Again, these accusations are unfounded. This work was led in Parliament by Wes Streeting, the current

Health Secretary and Anna Soubry, a barrister and former Conservative Defence and Veterans Minister. Both oppose blasphemy laws, as do I.

I've campaigned all over the world, including in Pakistan, against blasphemy laws and for those accused of blasphemy. These laws are often relics of a colonial past and embraced in more modern times by individuals seeking to establish and entrench their political power. They have little basis in Islam.

But it is also true that 'legitimate criticism' can often be used as a disguise for reinforcing stereotypes about a religion and stigmatising its followers, sometimes with deadly consequences.

Professor Tariq Modood, the founding director of the Centre of Ethnicity and Citizenship at the University of Bristol, presents a series of tests to determine whether what we are dealing with is reasonable criticism of Islam or Muslims, or Islamophobia. They provide a helpful prism for drawing a distinction between legitimate debate and targeted racism.

1. Does it *stereotype* Muslims by assuming they all think the same?
2. Is it *about* Muslims or a dialogue *with* Muslims, which they would wish to join in?
3. Is mutual learning possible?
4. Is the language civil and contextually appropriate?
5. Insincere criticism for ulterior motives?

The answers to these questions help frame Islamophobia or anti-Muslim racism.

I add my own test to this: swap the community and see if it still feels like an appropriate comment to make.

The debate about 'Muslim grooming gangs' is a good issue to subject to these tests. The central tenet is that, over a period of years, Muslim men in northern towns targeted 'white girls' for sexual exploitation and that this was somehow a behaviour rooted in their ethnic or religious identity.

It's an issue highlighted by the award-winning *Times* investigative journalist Andrew Norfolk. He was credited with uncovering a national scandal but there were serious problems in the racialised way he framed his findings. Concerns were also raised about Norfolk's portrayal of Muslims in other stories run by *The Times*, for example one scare story headlined on the front page 'Christian child forced into Muslim foster care' that on closer examination fell apart as a scandal.

The 'Muslim grooming gangs' issue was exploited by Stephen Yaxley-Lennon, aka Tommy Robinson, a convicted fraudster and stalker who has served multiple prison sentences. In 2019, he was jailed for nine months for contempt of court after filming himself outside Leeds Crown Court while a sexual crimes trial was ongoing. Two Old Bailey judges said he was stirring up 'vigilante action'.

In *Why I'm No Longer Talking to White People About Race*, Reni Eddo-Lodge asks why, when we discuss 'grooming gangs', we 'don't think that their [white male] actions are because of the deviancy of white men. When white men target babies, children and teenagers for sexual gratification, we don't ask for a deep reflection of these actions from the white male community', and yet 'men of colour's crimes are held up as evidence of the savagery of their race'.

Paedophilia has always tragically been a part of British society, as it has in all societies. Child abuse is an evil that we have been grappling with for centuries. Our response, now dealt with through the criminal justice system, was historically rooted in Christian morality: child abuse was seen as a perversion, a sin rather than a criminal act.

Historically, in the UK the age of consent was twelve until 1875, when it was raised to thirteen, and then to sixteen in 1885. I raise this because the age of consent for marriage in Islamic history (post-puberty) is often cited as a basis for child abuse being an exclusively Muslim problem. But that's as absurd as suggesting that Christianity has an inherent issue with child abuse because Mary was supposedly about fourteen years old when she was pregnant with Jesus.

A study published in 1958 by a female police surgeon found that of two thousand cases of child abuse in the UK between 1927 and 1954, half the victims were under the age of seven.

Back then, victim-blaming was commonplace. Those from poor backgrounds were not portrayed as innocent. Young girls particularly were viewed as somewhat culpable for the crimes committed against them, and often children above the age of thirteen were seen as having 'low morals' needing punishment and moral instruction rather than support.

It's an approach echoed by some of the perpetrators, seeing their victims as sexually available to them. And while racial slurs were used by some of the 'grooming gang' perpetrators, their victims were of all races.

Child abuse has been found in religious institutions, in schools, in sports clubs and children's homes. Celebrities, politicians, police officers and the military have, at times, been found to be systematically engaged in child sexual exploitation and abuse. Both boys and girls are abused, yet in the UK the perpetrators are overwhelmingly white men.

A 2022 report by the Centre of Expertise on Child Sexual Abuse, based on records of defendants prosecuted for child sexual abuse offences, concluded the vast majority were white: 89 per cent, while 6 per cent were Asian and 3 per cent were black.

Two years earlier, the Home Office's Group-based Child Sexual Exploitation Characteristics of Offending report found that 'based on the existing evidence . . . it seems most likely that the ethnicity of group-based CSE [child sexual exploitation] offenders is in line with CSA [child sexual abuse] more generally . . . with the majority of offenders being white'.

The Home Office report makes very clear that there are no grounds for asserting that Muslim or Pakistani-heritage men are disproportionately engaged in such crimes. It warned of 'potential for bias and inaccuracies in the way that ethnicity data is collected' with the possibility of 'greater attention being paid to certain types of offenders'.

This study was commissioned in 2018 by the then Home

Secretary Sajid Javid, who had famously tweeted, 'These sick Asian paedophiles are finally facing justice. I want to commend the bravery of the victims. For too long, they were ignored. Not on my watch. There will be no no-go areas.'

Javid, who was raised in a Pakistani Muslim home, says his 'family heritage is Muslim' but that he does 'not practise any religion'. Quite why he decided to tweet in such an inflammatory way we cannot say, but his own department's report found that there was no specific 'Asian paedophile' problem nor are there any 'no-go areas'.

Racist tropes are powerful; they can often be internalised by the very communities they seek to malign. Successive Home Secretaries initially refused to make the report public. Javid and Priti Patel claimed that publishing would not be in the public interest and suggested the report was for internal use only.

Clearly the facts and findings didn't support their rhetoric and weaponisation of the issue; the evidence didn't further their agenda so it could be ignored.

A Freedom of Information request and a public petition of more than 130,000 people asking for the report to be released led to Patel agreeing to publish. It took a further seven months and yet another change of Home Secretary for the report to at last be made public.

None of this is merely being over-sensitive. 'Groomer' has become a dangerous stereotype about Muslim men.

This toxic debate created a climate that resulted in the murder of Mohsin Ahmed, an eighty-one-year-old grandfather, in Rotherham in 2016 by two thugs as he made his way home from prayers. Dale Jones and Damien Hunt stomped on the elderly victim's head, causing fractured eye sockets and brain damage, while verbally abusing him and baselessly calling him a 'groomer'.

Brenton Tarrant also painted a reference to 'grooming' on his firearms when he slaughtered innocent Muslims in New Zealand. It's inspired far-right extremist groups; it is a campaign tool for the likes of the British National Party and English Defence League, as well as Reform UK.

There could be no greater public interest for the record to be set straight, for inaccurate tropes and stereotypes to be challenged by fact and evidence, and for the Home Secretary to publish a report that would hopefully make Muslim communities safer. The fact that Javid and Patel resisted, and only released the report after intense public pressure, shows how even in the government department tasked with protecting citizens Muslims Don't Matter.

Despite the tragic killing of Mohsin Ahmed, despite Home Office evidence that contradicted the notion of 'Muslim grooming gangs' being disproportionately represented in child sexual abuse cases, no lessons were learned, with Suella Braverman, like her predecessors Priti Patel and Sajid Javid, continuing to propagate and popularise notions of grooming gangs.

Braverman went even further, falsely asserting that group-based child sexual abuse was 'almost all British Pakistani men', a hugely divisive comment subsequently proven to be false and misleading, with the *Mail on Sunday* having to issue a correction.

A consortium of hundreds of leading British Pakistani business leaders, professionals and community groups wrote to Prime Minister Rishi Sunak in April 2023, asking for a meeting and for him to distance himself from Braverman's remarks. He did not even have the decency to acknowledge their complaint, let alone respond. The letter was sent on to the Home Secretary's department to mark her own homework. A follow-up letter was sent three months later, which received a response from a political adviser at No 10, rather than the PM. For Rishi Sunak, it seemed, Muslims Didn't Matter.

Mohsin Ahmed was not alone in being killed by a far-right attack in an atmosphere of hostility whipped up by politicians and the media. In 2013, Birmingham grandfather Mohammed Saleem was murdered a few hundred yards from his house as he walked home from the mosque by a far-right terrorist called Pavlo Lapshyn. After his arrest, Lapshyn was found to have planted bombs at mosques in Walsall, Wolverhampton and Tipton. The Tipton device was primed to explode during Friday prayers but due to a fortuitous change in prayer time the device exploded when the mosque was deserted. On searching Lapshyn's home, police found further bomb-making equipment.

Makram Ali, also a grandfather, was killed by far-right terrorist Darren Osborne, who ploughed his van into pedestrians outside the Muslim Welfare House in Finsbury Park, north London during the month of Ramadan in 2017. According to his estranged partner, Osborne had been radicalised by becoming 'obsessed' with a BBC docu-drama about a child sex abuse ring in Rotherham and blamed all Muslims.

Mohsin Ahmed, Mohammed Saleem, Makram Ali – all three men are victims of terrorism whose names appear to have been erased from the national consciousness. It seems that Muslims who are victims of terrorist attacks don't matter.

But these were men like my dad: grandfathers walking to or from the mosque for prayers, murdered simply for being Muslim. These attacks meant that I pleaded with my dad to no longer walk to the mosque in his hometown in West Yorkshire. He now travels by car for what would be a short walk and during late-night prayers is accompanied by a friend or family member.

Islamophobia has poisoned our streets, but it is also found in the most respectable settings: in think tanks, in editorial newsrooms, in the corridors of power and as conversation in polite society. It's a form of respectable racism, one that some have worn as a badge of honour. 'My own view is that there is not nearly enough Islamophobia within the Tory Party,' boasted the *Spectator* columnist Rod Liddle, and journalist Polly Toynbee has yet to denounce her 'I'm an Islamophobe – and proud of it' outburst from 1997.

The late journalist Christopher Hitchens, still a hero in many intellectual circles, once claimed that Islamophobia was 'only the objection to the preachings of a very extreme and absolutist religion'.

There is a sleight of hand in Hitchens's argument as he simplifies a fourteen-hundred-year-old spiritual tradition into something 'extreme and absolutist' to be dismissed out of hand and then labels any attempt to push back at his views as an affront to freedom of speech. It is, in fact, this very simplification, the narrowing of what Islam is to a set of objectionable practices or ideas, that is the very definition of Islamophobia.

The statement 'Islamophobia is a word created by fascists, used by cowards to manipulate morons', posted as a tweet in 2013, has been (mis)attributed to Christopher Hitchens by American Islamophobes Sam Harris and Bill Maher. It has been reposted millions of times on social networks and regularly makes an appearance on Muslims' timelines.

The truth is Islamophobia destroys lives and livelihoods. It is perpetuated by many with a vested interest in this form of racism being mainstreamed. It is unpopular to call it out and to do so in politics can be career-ending.

From the US to China, from the UK to India, it's a global issue, a worldwide epidemic, manifesting at worst as genocidal wars and internment camps and at its mildest as hijab-pulling and name-calling.

The seriousness of this phenomenon has been recognised by the United Nations, which warned in 2021 that 'Islamophobia builds imaginary constructs around Muslims that are used to justify state-sponsored discrimination, hostility and violence against Muslims with stark consequences for the enjoyment of human rights including freedom of religion or belief'.

As of 2022, the United Nations designates the date of the Christchurch Mosque terrorist attack, 15 March, the

UN International Day to Combat Islamophobia. Unlike many other UN International Days, the UK chooses not to mark it.

Islamophobia is Britain's bigotry blind spot.

And against this backdrop we continue to have arguments about the semantics of the word Islamophobia – battles over words have taken precedence over action to root out racism.

Even supposedly well-intentioned liberals have fallen into this trap. Former chair of the Equality and Human Rights Commission Trevor Phillips claimed in 2016 he had only seen one Muslim wearing a poppy at an event shortly before Remembrance Sunday. Many of the African and Eastern European industrial site workers he met on the same day, he said, *were* wearing poppies. It's seemingly beyond Phillips's comprehension that Africans and Eastern Europeans might be Muslim. This lazy stereotyping would be laughable were it not deeply hurtful for the many Muslims whose families served in the world wars, or who continue to serve in our armed forces.

Phillips has vehemently contended, on the one hand, that Muslims cannot be defined as a single race, so therefore cannot suffer racism, yet has himself repeatedly defined Muslims as a single group who 'are not like us'. He's said that Muslims may 'see the world differently from the rest of us'; he suggested that British Muslims are 'becoming a nation within a nation'; he has said, 'I thought Europe's Muslims would gradually blend into the landscape. I should have known better,' and argued that it was correct for

Muslims to be judged collectively. '[If] you do belong to a group, whether it is a church, or a football club,' he told the *Guardian*, 'you identify with a particular set of values, and you stand for it. And frankly you are judged by that.'

So, Muslims judged collectively according to Phillips is OK, but not protected collectively?

His comments earned the approval of Tommy Robinson and led to his suspension from the Labour Party. That suspension was quietly and without due process reversed by Keir Starmer's party shortly after Phillips was offered a Sunday morning political show on Sky and months before being awarded a knighthood having been nominated by Boris Johnson.

A Labour source told the *Guardian* at the time that the investigation into Phillips was ongoing, but I have to date found no evidence of this probe having been concluded and certainly it has not been made public. Anti-Muslim racism is as much a challenge for the left as it is for the right.

The deliberate obfuscation about what Islamophobia is and what it isn't is a calculated ploy to keep its normalisation in circulation without hindrance.

On 10 October 2023, referring to the 7 October attack by Hamas in Israel, Richard Ferrer, the editor of *Jewish News*, wrote, 'This is plain and simple historic Islamic bloodlust, passed down through the generations from birth.' This appalling racism repeated the equivalent of the antisemitic blood libel trope. After I challenged him, he changed the word Islamic to 'Islamist', and felt that was sufficient. Islamist is a fig leaf of a word with dozens of potential meanings; it is used by Islamophobes, who know most ordinary members of the public take it to mean simply 'Muslims'.

It was David Cameron, in his more enlightened days, who warned in 2007 that 'I try not to use phrases like "Islamist terrorist" because I think British Muslims read that and think, "He just means me." So, we are all trying to find a way through this language issue ... descriptions more accurate than those that were used in the past.'

The appalling stereotyping by Ferrer has had no consequences. He remains editor of *Jewish News* and continues to be a commentator on mainstream broadcast channels and to write in mainstream newspapers – because Muslims don't matter.

Just as the terms antisemitism and homophobia, despite not being linguistically impeccable, are used to indicate a variety of manifestations from discrimination to bigotry to violence against Jewish and LGBTQ+ individuals, so the term Islamophobia, similarly imperfect, can cover the same range of discriminatory manifestations.

This is not mere academic hair-splitting. The story of getting a Conservative government to acknowledge Islamophobia, define it and address it has been a long battle which I will explore in later chapters. But until all our political parties formally adopt the definition, as they have adopted the definition of antisemitism, we cannot fully tackle this latest scourge of racism to infect our shores. We cannot tackle what we dare not name.

In 2022, Aneil Karia and Riz Ahmed's powerful mix of cinematography, screenplay and rap *The Long Goodbye* dramatically illustrated the consequences of the normalisation of such hate.

This Oscar-nominated short film is uncomfortable but mandatory viewing. It juxtaposes extraordinary brutality with the ordinary everyday through the story of a far-right attack in a north London suburb.

It portrays the playfulness of a close-knit British Asian family preparing for a family wedding, a scene which for so many Muslims is warm, welcoming and familiar. Yet it ends in debilitating fear when young Asian men on their knees are shot in daylight by a far-right group while both the police and white neighbours ignore their cries for help.

Riz Ahmed uses rap and film to challenge current political narratives on identity and belonging and articulates the uneasy relationship and conflicting emotions that many Muslims feel in relation to their place in Britain today.

The film visualises the fear, anxiety and anger that many British Muslims have voiced to me. It shows the most brutal of hate crimes and what can happen when those tasked with protecting us fail. It's an uncompromising artistic reflection of Muslim fears – and a brutal depiction of what happens when Muslims don't matter.

.

2

The Rotten State

Frontline politics for Muslims is brutal. For me it has meant explaining to the Croydon Conservative Association why it wasn't a term of endearment to speak about the local 'Paki shop'. In this I had the support of the then parliamentary candidate for the area Gavin Barwell, now Lord Barwell, who was appalled by such expressions of prejudice.

It meant being monstered while party chairman by a now deceased MP at a meeting of the 1922 Committee of Tory grandees and being told, 'Young lady, you need to know your place.'

It meant being told to account for the simple good practice of notetaking in Cabinet. It meant one of my advisers being asked to keep an eye on me, despite my being a government minister and Privy Councillor. It meant being told not to refer the Policy Exchange think tank to an internal government extremism assessment after it had been found by a BBC *Newsnight* investigation to have relied upon fabricated evidence in its 2007 report 'The Hijacking of British Islam' – because it would upset a Cabinet colleague who was known for his Islamophobia.

And it's meant thousands of abusive and threatening emails, letters and messages that I now just accept as part of my daily inbox.

At a recent British Asian Trust event, a charity founded in 2007 by the then Prince of Wales to tackle poverty, inequality and injustice in South Asia, I was described as a 'one-woman Islamophobia rebuttal unit', an accolade of which I am proud, but I do bear the scars.

Politics has often felt like being in an abusive relationship, knowing it's not a good place to be but staying because the optimist in me thinks I can make it better for our kids' futures.

I also recognise that even in the midst of all this hostility, I still have privilege. The privilege of a platform in Parliament and the media, the freedom of no longer being on the front line of politics, the privilege of financial independence and, most importantly, the privilege of age and political knowledge. I have decided to exercise my privilege by speaking truth to power.

Having lived this journey and having sat at the table where decisions about Muslims were made, having had experience of the various individuals who perpetuate anti-Muslim policy and the multiple connections between them, seeing close up the personal and political journeys of today's generation of Islamophobes, acutely aware that coming generations of British people will ask how the hell did we let it get so bad, and a sickening worry that it could get even worse – all these reasons have compelled me to write this book.

My argument in this chapter is about those in power, those who control narratives and policymaking, those who hold sway and those who impact and shape the lives of communities. I can say what so many only dare to express behind closed doors. And I can say what I say about how those in power have failed British Muslims because I have seen it at first hand.

I am no longer prepared to listen to well-meaning colleagues who acknowledged the challenge but advised me not to speak out, urging me to keep my head down, convincing me that the environment would eventually change. It did not. The country my grandfathers fought for did not bow down to fascism a century ago and as once more we see bigotry rear its ugly head, I shall not do so today.

My Muslimness has been politicised against my will. I am not a Muslim who happens to be a politician, I am a politician who happens to be Muslim – and a woman, brown, straight, northern and working class. I have lost count of the number of times I've been asked the stupid and offensive question of whether I'm Muslim first or British first – a gotcha attempt at assessing my loyalty.

I am also a Conservative. I am a politician who believes in low tax, a small state; I believe in the safety net of a welfare state, that work should pay a minimum living wage and people should be able to keep more of what they earn. I believe in family and personal responsibility and individual liberty; and I believe in human rights, in evidence-led ethical and compassionate policymaking, and always trying to say what I believe and do as I say.

And yet the homogenisation of my Muslim identity by others is something that has preoccupied my political journey.

The war on terror was an early manifestation of how an undoubtedly complex issue quickly morphed into the othering of a whole community. Conversations on counter-terrorism became discussions about burkas and British values; national security legislation was drafted in terms that exceptionalised Muslims, with ramifications that we are still living with today.

Watching this policymaking up close – both with a seat at the table of power and a seat in the British Muslim community – I saw what in later years we would recognise as one of the first culture wars playing out in the UK. Its victims were British Muslims, and the state led the charge.

A cornerstone of this culture war was the government's policy of disengagement with the British Muslim community. This began in 2007 under New Labour, continued in the coalition years and was supercharged by the Conservatives – with the encouragement of right-wing think tanks and newspapers, which took to task British Muslims in ways no other community was subjected to.

Through the disengagement policy vast sections of Muslim civil society, particularly institutions rooted in communities, have been systematically maligned and excluded by successive governments. Both Labour and Conservative politicians have over a period of seventeen years cherry-picked or created new interlocutors from Muslim communities who do not question or challenge government – 'yes' men and women.

These yes-men (they are mostly men) have turned out to be problematic to say the least. In the Blair years, the government championed now defunct groups like the Quilliam Foundation, fronted by the former Hizb ut-Tahrir member turned anti-extremist campaigner and now anti-vaxxer Maajid Nawaz, who in 2022 abruptly left his radio station LBC after broadcasting his bizarre opinions; and the Sufi Muslim Council, set up by the failed parliamentary candidate Azhar Ali, who was stopped from standing for Labour in the 2024 Rochdale by-election after he made antisemitic remarks.

These individuals have disparagingly been referred to as 'native informants' but they are better described as opportunists. Presenting themselves as 'reformers', they have little or no influence to challenge or change Muslim communities from within. They are rarely seen courting actual Muslims (their supposed target audience) but in the case of Nawaz openly supported Islamophobe-in-chief Donald Trump. They are vociferously anti-free speech for Muslims but vociferously pro-free speech for Islamophobes.

I used to dismiss such figures as fools and irritants; I was naive to do so. Allowing them to frame the relations between Muslims and the state has been dangerous and disingenuous. During the coalition years, despite advice to the contrary from civil servants and others, Maajid Nawaz was invited by Michael Gove to attend Downing Street to brief David Cameron and Cabinet colleagues. Nothing new was learnt from the meeting but it allowed us to listen to Gove's views on Muslims through the mouth of a supposedly authentic voice.

The policy of disengagement also involved a concerted effort to freeze out and undermine the vibrant British Muslim charitable sector. The period between 2012 and 2018, when Sir William Shawcross was chair of the Charity Commission, saw a disproportionate focus on Muslim charities. More than a quarter of the statutory investigations launched within the first two years of his tenure targeted Muslim organisations. In the seventeen months from December 2012 to May 2014, the commission labelled fifty-five charities with the issue code 'extremism and radicalisation' without their knowledge, meaning they were monitored as a potential concern. Disturbingly, no written criteria existed for applying or removing this label; it was described by critics as 'non-evidence based' targeting of Muslim groups.

To give some context, Shawcross is a neoconservative journalist who in 2006 warned that 'We simply do not wish to face the fact that we really are threatened by a vast fifth column' of extremist Muslims. He served as a director of the right-wing think tank the Henry Jackson Society from October 2011 to September 2012, shortly after it had merged with the Centre for Social Cohesion, a think tank run by journalist Douglas Murray. This was the Douglas Murray who became infamous for declaring in his 2006 Pim Fortuyn speech that 'conditions for Muslims in Europe must be made harder across the board. Europe must look like a less attractive proposition.'

This policy of freezing out Muslims completely contrasted with the approach to other social groups: women, race groups, the LGBTQ+ community, Jewish communities and others. In all these cases, the government rightly made efforts to include a wide range of representation without interfering by favouring one set of interlocutors over another.

And yet in the case of Muslims, successive governments felt emboldened to determine the 'acceptable Muslims' – whether representative or not – based on whether they agreed with their often-biased policies towards Muslims and did not question any aspect of the UK's foreign policy in the Middle East. They were subject to approval by certain think tanks and even organisations from other faiths such as the Board of Deputies of British Jews, something that horrified me in government.

The outsourcing of these decisions to institutions with vested interests can lead to serious problems. In 2024, the taxpayer had to pay libel damages and costs on behalf of Michelle Donelan, then Secretary of State for Science, Innovation and Technology, who, based on advice from Policy Exchange, falsely accused an academic of being an extremist and supporting Hamas. Reports suggest that the legal advice and damages could cost the taxpayer up to £60,000.

Disengagement has meant that successive governments have stigmatised, isolated and, via a process of tenuous guilt by association, detached most mainstream British Muslim organisations and institutions from consultation and policymaking.

The demonisation starts early. Shaima Dallali was dismissed from her post as president of the National Union of Students in 2022 because of an alleged antisemitic post on Twitter in 2012, when she was a teenager and before she had even gone to university. Dallali regretted the tweet, admitted it was antisemitic and 'repeatedly apologised'. In May 2024 the NUS, having spent over £1 million on the investigation, settled Dallali's claim with a payment reportedly running into tens of thousands of pounds.

In November 2023 Baroness Foster, a Conservative peer, saw a young Muslim hijab-wearing woman appear on *University Challenge*. Foster tweeted that the Oxford astrophysics doctoral student Melika Gorgianeh should be arrested and expelled from university for wearing colours than resembled the Palestinian flag (in reality a navy blue, orange, green and pink jacket from Zara) and sitting near the team mascot: a blue octopus. Foster accused Gorgianeh (and only Gorgianeh) of choosing the mascot, which she said resembled an antisemitic trope. The Christ Church student received death threats because of the false accusations and she and her family felt fearful of leaving their home. Foster subsequently deleted the tweets, admitted the allegations were completely untrue, apologised and paid substantial damages and costs to Gorgianeh.

Young Muslims should not be forced to defend themselves legally against spurious allegations by powerful people.

Whether it's who we choose to represent us, who speaks for us, how we want to frame our issues, how we want to engage or how we are defined, when it comes to our relationship with power and decision-making, Muslims lack agency. We are not stakeholders. Policy is not something Muslims help to shape; it is weaponised as something done to us.

We are increasingly denied participation and forced to protest to be heard.

This is in stark contrast to how other communities are treated. Marie van der Zyl, then president of the Board of Deputies for British Jews, wrote to the government in March 2024 about rumours circulating suggesting the imminent removal of Lord Mann, the government's independent adviser on antisemitism. When talking about a potential replacement for Lord Mann, she said: 'I trust that you will consult with the Jewish community's democratic representative leadership and look to appoint through an open and transparent process an equally outstanding and non-controversial figure who will command respect from the vast majority of our community.'

This kind of opportunity is not afforded to British Muslims. Instead, there is no consultation with Muslim leadership, no open or transparent process for appointments. The people the government engages with, appoints or seeks advice from are most often controversial figures at the margins of British Muslim society, if a part of it at all. And unlike the Jewish community, British Muslims do not have the privilege of a government adviser on Islamophobia at all, never mind one that commands the respect of the vast majority of the country's four million Muslims.

In the Conservative Party leadership race of 2022, triggered by Boris Johnson's resignation, the *Daily Mail* even used Muslim engagement as a stick with which to beat one of the leadership hopefuls, Penny Mordaunt. They ran a story about a meeting held over a year earlier and already in the public domain between Mordaunt, a government minister, and Zara Mohammed, the first woman to be elected secretary-general of the Muslim Council of Britain, one of the largest Muslim umbrella organisations in the UK.

The *Mail* chastised Mordaunt for her 'dodgy judgment', in contrast to Liz Truss, whom they welcomed with high praise running the front page 'Cometh the hour, cometh the woman'. Forty-four days later, having crashed the markets, Truss went down in history as the shortest-serving prime minister in UK history. Truss has since taken to sharing platforms in the US with Islamophobes and conspiracy theorists.

The state's use of a counter-extremism lens through which to view all things Muslim has poisoned the government's relationship with Muslims – including cultural events such as Eid receptions at Downing Street, invitations to which are only extended to those who acquiesce to a 'state sanctioned' version of what Muslims should think.

This approach has resulted in flawed policymaking, stunted Muslim civil society development, left the best of the community out in the cold and tragically led to the development of an ill-informed nod-along Muslim for whom a samosa and a photo at No 10 is sufficient reward for their compliance. (Interestingly, in April 2024, in the middle of the Gaza onslaught and a government knee-deep in accusations of anti-Muslim racism, senior British Muslims from the worlds of business, arts, charity and politics did boycott the PM's Eid reception. Advisers at No 10 worked furiously to make up the numbers for an event which in the end was attended by few Muslims – and even fewer members of the government. Even Rishi Sunak failed to make an appearance.)

There is a particular irony to the tangle political leaders have got themselves in. On the one hand, the government insists on Muslims embracing 'fundamental British values' defined in the Prevent Strategy Document 2011 as 'democracy, the rule of law, individual liberty and mutual respect and tolerance of different faiths and beliefs'. But when Muslims challenge government on actions that detract from our commitment to the rule of law, for example torture or rendition; or challenge actions that undermine democracy, for example freedom of speech or freedom of association; or challenge actions that undermine respect and tolerance such as institutional Islamophobia; or challenge actions that undermine individual liberty such as the right of women to wear what they want – when Muslims apply fundamental British values such as exercising their democratic right to vote by electing MPs independent of party political constraints – they are demonised, marginalised, excluded from political arenas and treated as outcasts.

Years of being told the community is segregationist takes

on an even more Orwellian tone for those of us who chose participation (and encouraged others to do the same) and who are now faced with accusations of 'entryism'.

During my time in Cabinet, I was accused of just such 'entryism'.

As I sat in Cabinet and in the National Security Council, dealing with the aftermath of a terrorist attack and the murder of Lee Rigby in 2013, I was marked out to be treated with suspicion – Douglas Murray referred to me as 'the enemy at the table'.

A 2015 article by Andrew Gilligan in the *Telegraph* headlined 'Islamic "radicals" at the heart of Whitehall' utilised this trope too and sought to paint a cross-government working group on anti-Muslim hatred as an entryism plot instigated by me. The group had been set up in 2012 using the precedent of the cross-government group on tackling antisemitism, which had been founded in response to the recommendations in the 2006 All-Party Parliamentary Inquiry into Anti-Semitism and whose membership was selected by British Jewish community organisations.

Considering the government's policy of disengagement with almost every British Muslim community organisation, we sought to find credible and experienced individuals to take part. These included academics, public sector workers, a deputy lieutenant, individuals in receipt of honours, and someone who runs one of the largest international professional Muslim networks and works closely with the US State Department.

I was grateful these people stepped up and gave us their time pro bono. Gilligan's damaging article was eventually dismissed by the government in an official letter to each of the individuals named. The letter stated that 'none of the challenges to your integrity and the allegations in the article have any substance'.

To this day, some of those named in the *Telegraph* still travel with that official government letter because of concerns regarding airport stops and questioning triggered by such reporting. The article is still used by trolls on my social networks and makes a regular appearance on my timeline, accompanied by abuse.

The source of the article was Fiyaz Mughal, the director of Faith Matters and ex-director of Tell MAMA, which purportedly records anti-Muslim hate crimes, who early in 2024 was touted as the government's preferred candidate for an adviser on anti-Muslim hatred – until allegations emerged that he had suppressed a report detailing Conservative Party links to far-right and neo-Nazi organisations and individuals.

The Labour Mayor of London Sadiq Khan is the most high-profile British Muslim in politics. He has a long and well-documented history of being on the receiving end of hate because of his faith. (I recounted the history of Conservative Party smears and outright lies against Khan at length in my 2017 book, *The Enemy Within*.)

The latest smear came in February 2024. Lee Anderson, then deputy chairman of the Conservative Party, accused Khan of being controlled by 'Islamists' for not stopping protests calling for a ceasefire in Gaza. Having been asked to apologise and refusing to do so, Anderson had the Conservative whip withdrawn. He subsequently resigned from the party and joined Reform, for whom he is now an MP.

Had Anderson apologised, apparently there would have been no sanction. Watching the excruciatingly embarrassing interviews in the days after, where minister after minister refused to call out Anderson's comments as anti-Muslim racism, was a glimpse into the Tory mindset. The prime minister's mealy-mouthed reference to Anderson's remarks as merely 'wrong' and 'unacceptable' and 'ill judged' – refusing to call it Islamophobic or anti-Muslim – led to even Tory-sympathetic journalists finally calling it out. LBC presenter Nick Ferrari terminated an interview with Immigration Minister Michael Tomlinson mid-sentence when he repeatedly refused to call the comments Islamophobic.

Conservative political commentator Iain Dale said, 'I try . . . to put myself in the position of an ordinary British Muslim who hears these comments. And if I was an ordinary British Muslim, I would consider them Islamophobic without a shadow of a doubt.'

Iain and I have known each other for nearly two decades. We were both Tory parliamentary candidates in 2005. I've spoken to him in the past of the challenges of anti-Muslim racism in our party. He said in response to Anderson's comments, on BBC *Politics Live*, 'I used to think Sayeeda Warsi was going way over the top in some of her comments, but she's been proved right.' He also sent me a private message to say the same; it ended with 'Sorry'.

The message moved me to tears. A combination of anger that it had taken so long for others to see what I saw, but also relief that it had finally been seen. I called Iain to thank him.

Stigmatising and smearing Muslims in public life is no accident. It is a deliberate strategy designed to scare and silence British Muslims, to discourage them from taking their rightful place in public life and engaging with democratic and public institutions. It's about maligning character, damaging reputations and forcing Muslims out of the mainstream by ascribing to them ludicrous and often dangerous opinions.

In 2017, *Jewish News* published an article in which Richard Kemp, an ex-army officer who is now a regular GB News commentator, described me as an ISIS sympathiser. Ironically, this was at a time when I was on an ISIS kill list and had been given an extensive police protection plan.

I asked *Jewish News* to retract the article and Kemp's appalling comments. For months they refused to do so, treating my request with contempt. It took the appointment of solicitors and a legal battle for the article to be withdrawn and for a front-page apology to be issued. I donated the damages to interfaith and women's charities.

I'm far from the only one. Muslim schoolteacher and Labour councillor Nada al-Sanjari was falsely accused in several articles by Stephen Pollard, the editor of the *Jewish Chronicle*, and journalist Lee Harpin of launching and orchestrating a vicious campaign against a Jewish Labour MP.

Al-Sanjari was awarded a substantial sum in libel damages and legal costs, and both Pollard and Harpin apologised for what were 'completely unfounded allegations'.

Andrew Gilligan, who wrote the entryism story about me, cost the *Sunday Telegraph* substantial damages they paid for libel to Ifhat Smith, a mother who raised concerns about the treatment of her son at school under the government's Prevent counter-terrorism strategy, for falsely alleging she was an extremist.

The Times, *Telegraph*, *Mail* and *Express* paid libel damages and published apologies to a Muslim Scout leader, Ahammed Hussain, for false allegations of extremism made in 2019. The media attacks had begun with a *Daily Telegraph* investigation 'assisted' by the Henry Jackson Society.

The maligning of Muslims continues to this day. Lee Anderson made his comments on GB News, a media outlet started in 2021 with a promise to give a voice to the 'silenced' and 'sidelined'. It is part-owned by Paul Marshall, an evangelical Christian worth £800 million according to the *Sunday Times* Rich List and a Tory donor who donated to Michael Gove's 2016 leadership bid. The *Financial Times* has described him as 'an enthusiastic combatant in the UK's own version of America's culture wars'.

GB News's obsession with British Muslims is evidenced in a report by the Centre for Media Monitoring, which found the channel's coverage of 'grooming gangs' between 2 and 4 April 2023 was more than double that of all five mainstream news channels combined. Former *Newsnight* presenter Gavin Esler watched GB News for a month for an article in the May issue of *Prospect* magazine, and concluded that the channel pursued a 'one-note theme that Islam threatens our way of life'.

GB News has employed numerous sitting Conservative MPs and ex-ministers as hosts and commentators, and in October 2023 announced a flagship show for Boris Johnson, although that has yet to materialise.

It has given a platform to Mark Steyn, an enthusiast for the Eurabia conspiracy theory that Muslims are plotting to take over Europe. (He was sacked in 2023 after comments on the effectiveness of Covid vaccines.) In the eighteen months to March 2024, Ofcom found GB News guilty of twelve violations including breaches of the rules on due impartiality and a further seven investigations are still under way.

In February 2024 the anti-racism charity Hope not Hate exposed social media activity by Paul Marshall concealed behind an anonymised Twitter account, in which Marshall was repeatedly found to have liked and retweeted extremist content from an array of far-right and conspiracy theorist accounts. Marshall endorsed tweets from extreme Islamophobic and anti-migrant activists including notorious hate accounts such as the Britain First deputy leader Ashlea Simon. For example, he liked a post which said 'if we want European civilization to survive, we need to not just close the borders but start mass expulsions immediately. We don't stand a chance until we start that process very soon'. (A spokesperson for Marshall said his social media likes do not 'represent his views'.)

Marshall is also a founder of the children's charity ARK and until recently chairman of Ark Schools, one of the UK's leading providers of academies, which runs thirty-nine primary and secondary schools and twelve sixth forms. Marshall is currently bidding to buy the *Telegraph* and the *Spectator*. He is a powerful man with huge privilege and platforms. And he can, it seems, only grow more influential.

This stigmatisation of Muslim communities is not new. It is a deliberate dirty and dangerous game being played by some of the most powerful individuals in the media and at the top of politics, and it's relentless.

It has been drip fed over decades and it's no surprise that negative public polling about Muslims now reflects this. When prime ministers do not apologise for having spoken about Muslim women who wear face veils as 'bank robbers' or 'letter boxes'; when integration reviews (the Louise Casey Review of 2016) are predominantly about Muslims, even as anti-Muslim racism in society is rising; when national broadcasters can show programmes titled *What British Muslims Really Think* and use selective data to portray Muslims as uniquely not 'like us'; when think tanks can drive government policy despite their record of anti-Muslim hostility; when a newspaper columnist can get away with asking why a Muslim woman in a hijab is fronting a news report about a terrorist incident in France and get away with it (Fatima Manji was the presenter of Channel 4 News and the columnist the *Sun*'s Kelvin MacKenzie. The press regulator IPSO claimed 'The article did not include a prejudicial or pejorative reference to the complainant on the grounds of religion'); when *Woman's Hour* on BBC Radio 4 can post a video clip of hostile questioning of the first woman to lead a major British Muslim organisation as clickbait; when an ideologue with a documented history of anti-Muslim comments is selected to review counter-terrorism policy and pivots it to focus on 'Islamist' terrorism even as far-right and other ideologies account for the greater proportion of terrorism sympathisers (Sir William Shawcross and the 2023 Prevent Review), this is all deliberately creating suspicion and feeding hatred.

It is no coincidence, then, that Muslims are viewed less favourably than other religious groups: according to a University of Birmingham report on Islamophobia in 2022, 25.9 per cent of the British public feel negatively toward Muslims; this compares with 8.5 per cent for Jewish people and 6.4 per cent for black people. Gypsy and Irish Travellers are the least liked, at 44.6 per cent. More than one in four people, and nearly half of Conservative and Leave voters, hold conspiratorial views about Sharia 'no-go areas' promoted in the media; and a majority of Conservative voters also agree that 'Islam threatens the British way of life'.

British people are more confident in making judgements about Islam than other non-Christian religions but are much more likely to make incorrect assumptions about a complex and multi-faceted religion. Support for prohibiting all Muslim migration to the UK is at 18.1 per cent, higher than it is for other ethnic and religious groups (for Sikhs it's 11.8 per cent and 12 per cent for Jews). Trumpism is alive and well on these shores.

And despite attempts by politicians to pit Muslims against the 'white working class', people from the middle and upper classes are more likely to hold prejudiced views of Islamic beliefs than people from the working classes. Islamophobia is very much in evidence at the dinner tables of polite society.

A YouGov tracker on Islam and British values shows that almost consistently 50 per cent of British people feel 'There is a fundamental clash between Islam and the values of British society'. And it's not just the older generation. According to a survey of six thousand schoolchildren by the charity Show Racism the Red Card, nearly a third agreed with the statement 'Muslims are taking over England' and, shockingly, on average respondents thought Muslims made up 36 per cent of the population, as opposed to the true figure of around 6.5 per cent.

These widely held views have consequences: racism and exclusion at one end and physical and sometimes fatal attacks at the other.

We need to call out the hypocrisy of those who disguise their Islamophobia behind apparently legitimate concerns. The meat-eaters who have no qualms about the late-night kebab at a halal takeaway but who are suddenly vexed when Pizza Express announce their chicken was halal. The racist who suddenly becomes a defender of the countryside when he sees Muslim hikers. Where bigots compare Muslim walkers to the 'Serengeti wildebeest migration' and want Britain's wonderful hiking trails to be no-go areas for Muslims.

The secular Richard Dawkins who is 'horrified' by

twinkly fairy lights that celebrate Ramadan on Oxford Street but who also sees Christianity as 'a fundamentally decent religion in the way Islam is not'. The outrage in the right-wing media triggered by Ramadan lights would be hilarious if it were not so disturbing. Alex Phillips, a former Brexit Party Member of the European Parliament and now a television presenter, referred to them on Talk TV as signalling a 'creeping erosion of Christianity' with Islam being 'forced down our throats'.

Then there are those white men projecting themselves as champions of Muslim women's rights. Usually sceptical of feminism, these white saviours only speak up if the fight is against 'Islamic' men, not when we fight Islamophobic men. These men have short memories, convincing themselves that misogyny is a foreign, Muslim construct, forgetting our own recent history of women being denied choice, the right to vote, to work and own property. Such men love to talk of empowering us, but label empowered Muslim women as difficult, pushy and not knowing their place.

Even the well-intentioned paternalists can make embarrassing misjudgements, as when David Cameron was reported to have said in private that young men could become radicalised because of the supposed 'traditional submissiveness of Muslim women'. In response, some hilarious memes made by high-achieving Muslim women went viral.

And even in liberal spaces like the feminist movement, Muslim women are often spoken about, spoken at, or frozen out. There has been a near deathly silence from feminists in the corridors of power as the young Labour MP Zarah

Sultana, officially one of the most abused parliamentarians, continues to live with threats to her life. Her numerous emotional pleadings on the floor of the Commons, asking those in power to stop the vilification of Muslims, have fallen on deaf ears.

During a parliamentary debate on Israel and Gaza in January 2024, Sultana asked Rishi Sunak if he would 'seek to de-escalate the situation and call for an immediate ceasefire'. The prime minister fired back at her: 'Perhaps the honourable lady would do well to call on Hamas and the Houthis to de-escalate the situation.' Sunak's response was an attempt to delegitimise both Sultana's political point and perpetuated a trope that she, as a Muslim, was somehow connected to or had a special way of getting through to Hamas and the Houthis. The Labour leadership did not demand an apology, nor did Labour feminists line up to defend Sultana: it was left to another Muslim Labour female MP to raise the issue as a point of order with the PM and ask him to apologise.

It seems that on the issue of Islamophobia, even some Labour feminists have a blind spot. To quote Reni Eddo-Lodge again: 'Feminist activists would be foolish to ally with political forces that only ever speak in defence of women when there are Muslims to bash.'

The conflict in Gaza has, for many, crystallised just how little Muslim lives matter to the those in the corridors of power. The killing of tens of thousands of innocent civilians; the misrepresentation of Palestinians as all 'Islamists' or 'extremists'; the seeming ignorance that the oldest Christian community in the world is under attack in the land where Jesus was born; and the ex-Home Secretary Suella Braverman's concerted efforts to malign ethnically and religiously diverse antiwar protestors asking for a ceasefire as 'valorising terrorism' and 'hate marches' – all these smears were possible because the Palestinian cause is associated with Muslims.

Braverman and her media enablers knew that blaming Muslims was an effective strategy because Muslims, in our political culture, do not matter. As the death toll passed thirty thousand, as the UN warned of famine, and as millions across the world took to the streets week after week to try to stop the killing, it took the tragic death of three white British men, former soldiers guarding aid workers in Gaza, for the tone to change – if only for a few days.

Having defined Palestinians as 'Muslims', we made them subhuman, their deaths unimportant, their stories of suffering unworthy of front pages. They didn't deserve a refugee evacuation programme, or a family reunion scheme as had been implemented for Ukrainians. The Home Office even refused to evacuate children suffering the most horrendous injuries. Politicians couldn't even find the words to describe their humanity. Palestinian babies and toddlers did not even deserve to be called innocents. It was the starkest and most brutal wake-up call that even when individuals may not actually be Muslim, once racialised as such they no longer matter.

3

The Dinner Table Test

While in government, I first started sounding the sirens of concern in a 2011 speech about how Islamophobia was 'passing the dinner table test'. This was the first time a major speech on anti-Muslim prejudice had been made by a Cabinet minister, let alone the Conservative Party chairman. At the time, muscular liberalism and attacks on multiculturalism had started to infect Conservative politics. A party that had prided itself on individual liberty, freedom of speech and freedom of religion found itself setting a prescriptive and illiberal vision for British Muslims.

I found this change troubling because I had been a part of the optimistic early Cameron years. There was a commitment to get language right, a questioning of neoconservative ideology and a concerted effort to engage openly, honestly and authentically. Let me quote David Cameron from

2006: 'We must not stoop to illiberalism – whether at Guantánamo Bay, or here at home with excessive periods of detention without trial. We must not turn a blind eye to the excesses of our allies – abuses of human rights in some Arab countries, or disproportionate Israeli bombing in Lebanon. We are fighting for the principles of civilisation – let us not abandon those principles in the methods we employ.'

Post the Blair years of patronising engagement and caustic language which had started the process of vilification of British Muslims, I genuinely felt we could step away from the neoconservative ideology imported from the US that New Labour had become enamoured with.

I have talked to many Cabinet ministers and advisers from the New Labour years who have spoken candidly of the ideological rot that had set in regarding this policy area. It was not until the late years of the Labour government under Gordon Brown that some sanity was restored.

The early Cameron years were getting things right. When I looked at the ways in which European counterparts purported to uphold liberty by banning headscarves in classrooms and burkinis on the beach, banning minarets and even calling for bans of religious texts, I felt proud that when flashpoints appeared – like when Labour Cabinet minister Jack Straw made an uninvited visit to Muslim women's closets in 2006, saying he felt 'uneasy talking to someone' wearing a face veil – my colleagues seemed instinctively to fall on the right side of the argument.

But soon I saw this creeping 'muscular liberalism' approach up close and first hand. (A more detailed version of what follows is documented in *The Enemy Within*, in the chapter 'The Paranoid State'.) In a nutshell, policymaking started to exceptionalise the way we engaged with, viewed and judged British Muslims: they were held to higher standards than everyone else.

Ideological crusader Cabinet colleagues like Michael Gove, for whom fact and expert evidence was simply an irritating distraction, fed the frenzy of bad policymaking rooted in a new socially respectable form of prejudice, the kind casually discussed around the dinner table.

Much has been written about my 'dinner table' reference, but it's important to recall the principal arguments. First, the bifurcation of Muslims into 'moderates' and 'extremists', a clumsy and theologically unsound designation foisted upon a British Muslim community of four million and a worldwide community of nearly two billion. Since then, the language has changed: the talk is now of 'Islamist' and 'non-Islamist', but the connotations are the same. Islamist, a word with a dozen potential meanings, is often a fig leaf used by Islamophobes to disguise their bigotry.

My second point was the discomfort around those who devoutly observe Islam as opposed to those who wear their faith lightly. Third was the leaking of Islamophobic discourse into mainstream politics and the media via think tanks, journalists and politicians under the guise of challenging orthodoxies around institutionalised religion and protecting freedom of speech. Last was the exceptionalising of Muslims to demarcate them as somehow different from other groups.

I have often been asked why I felt it necessary to make that speech, given its political riskiness. In many ways it marked my political card. But I did so because the silencing, stigmatising and stereotyping of British Muslims was and still is stifling communities; its corrosive impact on public discourse and opinion is real; if we continue on this path the end point will be catastrophic.

It's important to note that this is not led by the British people themselves. In fact, what gives me hope are the positive everyday encounters between Muslims and non-Muslims, which develop organically and are thus more resilient. But we are being misled by individuals who pose as patriots and behave like arsonists. Spewing hateful anti-Muslim ideology, they are literally setting our country alight. They lead the charge against Muslims alongside the battle to discredit multiculturalism, despite many of them being the positive by-products of multiculturalism themselves. Multiculturalism has not and is not failing in this country – but there is a deliberate and concerted attempt by some to not let it succeed.

In government, Islamophobia has become hardwired. In today's Conservative Party, it has even targeted those like my colleague Nusrat Ghani, who at first did not rock the boat, indeed even went as far as sharing platforms with individuals who undermined the work to challenge anti-Muslim racism. Despite her initial acquiescence, though, she found herself removed from her ministerial role, with the then chief whip allegedly advising her to tone down her 'Muslimness' – in other words, she was sacked for being perceived to be too Muslim. (Mark Spencer, the chief whip in question, has responded saying that 'I have never used those words attributed to me'.)

The result is a closing of the political space for British Muslims in mainstream politics, where you must be the 'right kind of Muslim' just to survive, never mind succeed. Afraid of speaking out for fear of being marginalised and marginalised because we remained silent – this is a lesson Nusrat learned all too painfully. This has had a chilling effect, with many young Muslims entering politics sanitising, even denying, their 'Muslimness'.

This self-sanitising has crept into many aspects of life, for example Muslim parents opting for non-Muslim-sounding names to make their children's futures less challenging. A 2018 investigation by the *Sun* found that motorists named Mohammed were being charged up to £919 more in car insurance than men with names like John Smith. A 2017 BBC investigation similarly found that candidates with Muslim-sounding names were three times more likely to be passed over for jobs.

We live in a time where we encourage people to be true to themselves. 'You do you' has become a popular phrase, but 'you doing you' when expressing your Islamic identity is not easy. Islamophobia suffocates authenticity.

You cannot tackle what you do not define yet attempts to define Islamophobia have consistently been sabotaged over the last decade. From attacks on individuals working in this area to pseudo-academic arguing over the term

Islamophobia, from the exclusion of civil society organisations to the leaking and briefing from government departments to certain think tanks working hand in glove with ministers, to the feeding of false information to the National Police Chiefs Council, to outright lies published in reports and newspapers – the campaign to silence and stop this work has been ferocious.

The last Conservative government continually flip-flopped on its official position. In 2010, the government argued we did not have the data to show Islamophobia was a problem. Two years later it was presented with statistics which showed it was a real and growing issue, and accepted it was indeed a problem. But then they argued that government didn't need a definition to tackle Islamophobia. When they eventually accepted the need for a definition, they said it would need to be decided by consensus.

Years went by with no action. Eventually, the All-Party Parliamentary Group on British Muslims took it upon themselves to start an inquiry, of which I was a part. After one of the most in-depth pieces of work led by parliamentarians in this area, the group reached the agreed definition cited in Chapter 1: 'Islamophobia is rooted in racism and is a type of racism that targets expressions of Muslimness and perceived Muslimness.' More than eight hundred Muslim organisations and institutions, from traditional to secular, supported the definition; it was underpinned by over eighty academic specialists and framed by a cross-party group of parliamentarians after a large countrywide consultation and evidence-gathering process including victim testimonies. And yet the government refused to adopt it.

The government said it wanted an agreed definition, just not one, it seems, agreed to by British Muslims, the community that the definition would seek to protect. Instead, the government announced it would appoint two advisers who would find a new definition. They only ever appointed one, Qari Asim, a legal director at the law firm DLA Piper and a senior imam. He was given no terms of reference, no resources and no ministerial engagement. Michael Gove, as Communities Secretary, cited Asim's role in the Commons when promoting the government's work to stamp out discrimination against Muslims but, like No 10, he at no point engaged with him. Asim's emails and letters went unanswered and three years later Gove unceremoniously dismissed him via a letter in the media.

But here is the good news. Despite all this game-playing, the Islamophobia definition has been adopted by all mainstream political parties bar the Conservatives (though the Conservative Party in Scotland had adopted it). It's also been supported by the mayors of London and Greater Manchester, and by sixty-five local authorities.

A party of government failing Muslims in this way is deeply worrying, but what makes this particularly disturbing is that at the time the Conservative Party was itself mired in allegations of Islamophobia dating back to at least 2015. Hundreds of incidents within the voluntary and parliamentary party raised with successive party chairmen and prime ministers were simply not taken seriously.

Islamophobia and antisemitism exist across political parties. The Labour Party has many examples of where even the so-called liberal left have failed to understand and tackle these forms of racism. On the issue of antisemitism under the leadership of Jeremy Corbyn, Labour found itself sanctioned by the Equalities and Human Rights Commission.

The Conservative Party, knowing full well its internal issues on anti-Muslim racism, sought to distract by focusing on anti-Jewish racism in Labour. It was deeply hypocritical of them. When the fight against racism is fought not on principle but on political opportunism, we are in dangerous territory. The contradiction of fighting antisemitism while perpetuating anti-Muslim racism – picking winners and losers among communities – was an appalling weaponisation of racism for political purposes.

Four years after the Conservative Party first started receiving complaints of Islamophobia, the party was finally bounced into agreeing to a review by Sajid Javid during the June 2019 leadership debates. I remember watching with shock as each contender agreed to a review when asked by Javid to do so.

This moment came a week or so after Javid, then Home Secretary, had been excluded from the state banquet held in honour of President Trump. His request to attend was rejected by No 10. He was the only holder of a great office of state not to attend and far more junior ministers were present. The Radio 4 interview in which he is asked about the snub is a moving and difficult listen. His realisation that he may have been excluded for his religious background could well have been the trigger to demand an inquiry.

Javid's short message to me after the debates – 'Right. Sorted out that Con Party Islamophobia investigation' – showed a glimpse of the kind of politician he could have been, as opposed to the citizenship-stripping, inflammatory-tweeting version he publicly projected.

In December 2019, the new prime minister Boris Johnson duly appointed Professor Swaran Singh to lead the inquiry. Singh, who is not Muslim, is a first-generation migrant from India with historic familial links to the disputed region of Kashmir. He has written in the past of how he views this personal loss: 'Indian Kashmir has now almost been cleansed of its non-Muslim population; my clan, a successful minority in Kashmir, has been without a home for three decades.'

Human rights abuses, extrajudicial killings, rape as a weapon of war and other atrocities against the civilian population of Kashmir are well documented by the UN. Yet in a 2019 article Singh sought to paint Kashmiri Muslims as having a victim mentality, just as he thought the Palestinians did, and complained 'Kashmiri Sikhs and Pandits do not meet the criteria of victimhood. Kashmiri Hindus can't be considered victims because they are, well, Hindus.'

Singh's article appeared in *Spiked*, an online publication whose then editor Brendan O'Neill had argued that '"Islamophobia" is an elite invention, a top-down conceit, designed to chill open discussion about religion and values and to protect one particular religion from blasphemy'.

Moreover, Singh had been asked to lead an inquiry into an organisation facing accusations of institutional racism – the Conversative Party – yet had previously argued that the concept of institutional racism doesn't exist.

Equally compromised was Wasiq Wasiq, an associate fellow of the Henry Jackson Society, who was appointed to the inquiry as a lay adviser. Wasiq had previously written for *Spiked* saying 'we need to junk the idea of "Islamophobia"' and arguing that it feeds a grievance narrative.

Singh's inquiry failed to interview complainants and, despite being presented with detailed evidence of Islamophobic comments and actions, simply failed to follow the facts. It did not take testimony from senior Muslim Conservative parliamentarians like former MEP Sajjad Karim, Muslim councillors, or volunteers. It did take evidence from Nusrat Ghani, but she subsequently refused to allow it to be used in the report because of the contempt with which she was treated by the inquiry and Singh's refusal to follow up her complaints.

On the day I was invited to give evidence, I found out my dad had contracted Covid. I started to record the session but was told it wasn't necessary as they would furnish me with a recording. I relied on this assurance in good faith, but it was reneged on. (They subsequently offered their transcript.) The whole experience made me feel like I was in the dock for having the audacity to call out racism. Singh made the session unnecessarily personal, asking me to explain my views on him. I told him he was prejudicing the inquiry by his approach, that this wasn't about him or me but about the issues, and I urged him to follow the evidence. The uncomfortable exchange eventually ended when another panellist intervened.

The inquiry found that two thirds of *all* complaints to the party were allegations of anti-Muslim discrimination. The impression was that the party and its leadership were insensitive to Muslim communities and that the complaints process lacked transparency. Despite reams of evidence, though, the inquiry somehow found that the party was not institutionally racist. And no consequences followed, even for those whom the report found had perpetuated anti-Muslim racism in the party.

This whitewash of a report did not garner the support, confidence or consent of any Muslim party member or Conservative Muslim parliamentarians.

Despite this, my colleagues continued to attack Labour for antisemitism. The approach was fascinatingly hypocritical. It seemed the Conservative Party's desire to root out racism was both limited to the Labour Party and limited to anti-Jewish racism. The Conservative Party has yet to take the Labour Party to task, for example, on the issue of its Islamophobia.

Labour certainly has its own anti-Muslim problem. Despite having received 85 per cent of the Muslim vote in the 2019 election, it has failed to adequately respond to anti-Muslim racism experienced by its members.

Reports of the Labour Party banning its councillors and MPs from attending pro-Palestinian marches (but not pro-Israel marches) displayed yet again what the 2022 Forde

Report on racism within the party, commissioned by Keir Starmer, referred to as the 'hierarchy of racism'.

The year after the report came out its author Martin Forde, KC, lamented that 'anti-black racism and Islamophobia are not taken as seriously as antisemitism'. It was a view reinforced by an Al Jazeera investigation called *The Labour Files*, broadcast a few months after the publication of the Forde Report, which revealed 'how a British political party that claims to embrace progressive values created a hierarchy of racism that discriminated against its Black, Asian and Muslim members'.

This had also been expressed during the Batley and Spen by-election in 2021 by an off-the-record senior Labour official telling the *Mail on Sunday* columnist Dan Hodges that 'We're haemorrhaging votes among Muslim voters, and the reason for that is what Keir has been doing on antisemitism'. The Labour Muslim network described the comments as 'a patently vile, Islamophobic briefing' in assuming Muslims dislike work combating antisemitism.

In October 2023, during conversations between the Labour leadership and concerned councillors on the issue of Israel and Gaza, a well-known national executive member was reported to have dismissed resignations by councillors over Labour's position as 'shaking off the fleas'.

This hierarchy of racism became an issue during the 2024 general election campaign. Trevor Phillips's suspension in 2020 for alleged Islamophobic comments had been quietly dropped without a concluded inquiry or an explanation. But Diane Abbott and Kate Osamor, both under investigation for alleged antisemitism, continued to languish in no man's land with no inquiry, no process, no timeline within which their cases would be considered, and no quiet exoneration.

Both Osamor and Abbott were finally readmitted to the party, Abbott at the eleventh hour, just days before candidate nominations were due to close. But the damage was done. It seems that in Labour, to be Islamophobic is forgivable; to be accused of antisemitism, as Faiza Shaheen, the former Labour candidate for Chingford and Woodford Green discovered when she was dismissed for, among other things, liking a Jon Stewart sketch about the Israel lobby on Twitter, is career-ending.

Having spent the last three decades as a racial justice campaigner, one of the hardest things for me has been to call out racism when it's perpetuated by other people of colour and other minorities. The stereotyping of a community, using racial tropes and the exceptionalising of them in politics, is not the preserve of white people. Brown and black and Jewish people can be racist too.

In April 2023, in the middle of the Braverman Pakistani grooming gang furore, LBC presenter James O'Brien asked me whether Suella Braverman was racist for the language she was using about the Pakistani and Muslim community. I answered that racism among minority communities is visible around the world and has led to horrendous consequences, for example the anti-Muslim racism practised by extremist Buddhists in Burma and Sri Lanka that led to the slaughter of Muslim minorities.

Anti-Muslim racism is at the core of extreme Hindutva

ideology, openly on display during the Indian elections in 2024, and has led to extreme violence against Indian Muslims, including lynchings for eating beef or for marrying a Hindu.

Similarly, the extreme anti-Arab, anti-Palestinian and anti-Muslim racism displayed by some in the Jewish community during Israel's attack on Gaza has been deeply disturbing. For me this has been particularly alarming, because of the Jewish community's own history of facing racism in Europe.

In October 2023, Jake Wallis Simons, the editor of the *Jewish Chronicle*, tweeted 'We need to face reality: much of Muslim culture is in the grip of a death cult that sacralises bloodshed' – referencing nearly two billion people worldwide, all of whom who have very different and distinct cultures.

After I and others challenged him, he deleted his tweet, yet continues to write biased and divisive pieces, remains editor and continues to inhabit mainstream broadcast and print platforms including the BBC. No consequences flow for Islamophobia because Muslims Don't Matter.

Anti-Arab and anti-Muslim racism in Israel and the occupied Palestinian territories has over recent months been on open display with the rantings of senior members of the Israeli government, sections of its military and among the illegal settler communities. It's the rhetoric that has led to the extreme violence and dehumanisation of the Palestinian people who have been killed in their thousands by Israeli bombs.

This was the racism that I was subjected to by the *Jewish News* writer who absurdly claimed I was an ISIS supporter. It is the racism I was subjected to in government when I was singled out for blame by Conservative Friends of Israel for a Foreign Office admin error, signed off by Middle East Minister Alistair Burt on the number of Palestinian deaths in a specific period. It's the racism I refer to regularly on *A Muslim and a Jew Go There*, the podcast I present with author and comedian David Baddiel, when I express my deep hurt at being subjected to racism by a community which should know better than to perpetuate it against a fellow minority.

Islamophobia is a form of racism that targets expressions of Muslimness or perceived Muslimness. Being subjected to it has nothing to do with the colour of one's skin; and the colour of one's skin is not a determinant factor in those that perpetrate Islamophobia and anti-Muslim racism either.

4

Unpopular Culture

The 1970s sitcoms *Mind Your Language* and *It Ain't Half Hot Mum* were compulsory viewing in our home. As a child, I recall my parents watching both programmes and laughing at the performance of actor Dino Shafeek, a British Bengali who had immigrated to England in 1958 from Dhaka, now the capital of Bangladesh.

Viewed through today's lens, Shafeek's characters – Ali Nadim, a Muslim migrant from Lahore in *Mind Your Language* and Chai Wallah Muhammed in *It Ain't Half Hot Mum* – were supposed to provoke laughter at Muslims rather than with them. And yet for my parents the mere fact that brown Muslims were reflected on our national screens, however poorly, was better than nothing.

This raises the real complexities of both why seeing yourself on screen matters and the various stages representation passes through before it becomes authentically recognised and appreciated by the people being represented.

Complaints about how minorities are presented on screen are, these days, very common, especially on social media. On the release of Christopher Nolan's biopic *Oppenheimer* in 2023, much was made of the fact that Robert Oppenheimer and Einstein, both Jewish, were played by non-Jews: Cillian Murphy and Tom Conti respectively. It reignited the debate about what is called 'Jewface': non-Jews impersonating Jews on screen.

The debate is not new. Jewface was originally used to describe the stereotyping and dehumanising of Jewish people on stage and in film. This was similar to the way blackface had been used: 'displaying Blackness for the enjoyment and edification of white viewers', according to John Strausbaugh, author of *Black Like You: Blackface, Whiteface, Insult & Imitation in American Popular Culture.* (For example, in the long-running BBC programme *The Black and White Minstrel Show.*) A famous example of Jewface was Alec Guinness's performance as Fagin in the 1948 film adaptation of *Oliver Twist*, complete with long prosthetic nose and lisping accent, which was criticised even at the time for being antisemitic.

At their core, such performances had racial animus. But in recent years the Jewface debate has moved on from concerns about negative tropes to concerns about non-Jews merely playing Jews. For his performance as the conductor Leonard Bernstein in the 2023 film *Maestro*, the non-Jewish actor Bradley Cooper wore a prosthetic nose that some deemed offensive. But the sympathetic portrayal, which won Cooper the support from Bernstein's relatives as well as an Oscar nomination, was a world away from the stereotypes of previous eras.

From a Muslim's perspective, the *Oppenheimer* and *Maestro* furores feel like a bit of a first-world problem. Our worry isn't whether Muslim actors get to play great Muslim roles. We're too busy fighting for any portrayal of any positive Muslim character by any actor *at all*. We might have moved on from *Mind Your Language*, but not nearly so far as we should have done.

Jack Shaheen, an Arab American author and US army veteran, produced a body of work evidencing anti-Arab and anti-Muslim stereotyping in American popular culture. In his book *Reel Bad Arabs: How Hollywood Vilifies a People*, he documented common stereotypes starting with the belly dancer, the rich sheikh and the barbaric Arab, right through to the pre- and post-9/11 savage Muslim terrorist. He concluded that 'Arabs are the most maligned group in the history of Hollywood'.

For most of my adult life, the only Muslims I ever saw on screen were the angry, repressive patriarch, the submissive woman, the religious fanatic, or the terrorist. Hollywood action films like Arnold Schwarzenegger's 1994 *True Lies* with British actor Art Malik's portrayal of the leader of terrorist organisation Crimson Jihad was an early example of a 'comic' terrorist.

After 9/11 there was an explosion of movies portraying American violence inflicted on Arabs or Muslims who were often a sinister, malevolent but mostly absent presence. These included *The Hurt Locker*, set during the Iraq occupation, *Zero Dark Thirty*, about the assassination of Osama bin Laden, and, most starkly, *American Sniper*. All three films were based on true events and showed the brutality of the war on terror in an essentially heroic light. They were acclaimed for their authentic representation of conflict, won awards and were watched by millions. Yet in each one the Muslim was the other, the enemy, a dehumanised figure not deserving of sympathy, never mind an authentic depiction of their experience on the receiving end of US power.

A 2017 master's thesis by Marloes Veldhausz on these three movies found that the stories, characters and even the style in which the movies were made all played into Islamophobic tropes. The use of camera shots, filming angles and positioning of characters, it is argued, added to the experience of othering their Muslim and Arab characters. Veldhausz found that 'because [these films] focus on events post-9/11, the ideological markers that trigger Islamophobia in these movies are thus related to the opinions on Islam that have become widespread throughout Hollywood and the media since. Muslims are seen as the universal Other [. . .] They are portrayed as non-compatible with Western societies, savages, evil, terrorists, and a threat to everything that Western societies hold dear.'

This stereotyping and stigmatising of a whole community demonises Muslims and Arabs and perpetuates Islamophobia, Veldhausz argues; if applied to a different group 'such as Jews or Asians' it would lead to 'widespread outrage'.

Islamophobia and anti-Muslim threats were reported by the *Guardian* to have tripled after the release of *American Sniper* in January 2015, prompting the American Arab Anti-Discrimination Committee to write to Bradley Cooper, who played the US sniper on duty in Iraq who kills a woman and a child, and the film's director Clint Eastwood, asking them to speak out 'in an effort to help reduce the hateful rhetoric'. Comments on social networks such as 'great fucking movie and now I really want to kill some fucking ragheads' and 'american sniper makes me wanna go shoot some fuckin arabs' were widely shared.

American Sniper divided Hollywood, film critics and politicians. Some called it a 'scandalously blinkered propaganda film'; others saw it a true depiction of a clean-cut all-American hero. Some questioned its political aims, given it was directed by the prominent Republican Eastwood – who claimed, implausibly, that it was 'the biggest antiwar statement'. But whatever its director's intentions, the film played a part in framing a negative narrative on Muslims and Arabs. As author Jordan Elgrably wrote, in *American Sniper* 'it seems that the only good Iraqi is a dead Iraqi'.

The hit US drama series *Homeland* also faced criticism for its clichéd Muslim and Arab characters, who were presented either as terrorists or as collaborators in the war on terror. Equally offensive were its stereotyping of whole communities, the tropes it perpetuated about Western Muslims as potential traitors and its bizarre depictions of well-developed cities like Islamabad in Pakistan as war zones.

At the time of its release, I was the UK Minister for

Pakistan, and was embarrassed by its hilariously inaccurate depiction of Western diplomacy there. What was even more hilarious, though, was how Arab street artists, hired to graffiti a film set to make it look like an authentic Syrian refugee camp, took their revenge by writing '*Homeland* is racist' and '*Homeland* is a joke' in Arabic.

Film and TV are powerful mediums. They can entertain, inspire and introduce us to a kaleidoscope of emotions. They have the power to frame the good guys versus the bad, influence our allegiances and sympathies, determine what we normalise as acceptable, direct us to whom we should loathe and whom we should love. They are powerful vehicles for propaganda that can pave the way for divisive politics and policymaking and create the backdrop which allows society to ignore the human rights of certain unfashionable groups.

It isn't just the US. In India there have been recent collaborations between the extreme right Hindu nationalist political party, the BJP, the Narendra Modi government and Bollywood. Anti-Muslim Bollywood movies have been hugely popular. *The Kashmir Files* (2022) and *The Kerala Story* (2023) both have anti-Muslim storylines, described by critic Kaashif Hajee as 'a new kind of unabashedly bigoted blockbuster'. Both received concessions from BJP-ruled states in the form of tax exemptions on ticket sales to boost the number of viewers and paid leave for civil servants to allow them to watch the movies.

Article 370, another Kashmir-focused movie, grossed over 1.1 billion rupees worldwide and was endorsed by Modi, although some critics called it 'thinly veiled propaganda'.

Some of the dialogue in the film echoed the controversial BJP Home Minister Amit Shah's speech in Parliament. Amit Shah, who has called Muslims 'infiltrators' and 'termites', was reappointed to his role by Modi after the Indian election in June 2024.

The ability and willingness of film and TV to propagate a negative discourse about Muslims is not innocent and has real-life consequences.

Sam Singh Gill, CEO of the US-based philanthropic organisation the Doris Duke Foundation, articulated this in February 2024: 'Monochromatic depictions of our society combined with stereotyping and villainization of difference are problematic in and of themselves. But they are made worse by how they inflame rather than soothe episodes of division and discord in our society.' He raised concerns about the effect of these depictions, including 'increased rates of harassment and physical violence' being reported by both Muslims and Jews in the US.

The drip-feeding of negative stereotypes isn't confined to action movies. Comedy can also exploit lazy negative tropes.

British comedian Sacha Baron Cohen has been particularly prolific in this area. His portrayal of his character Borat as a misogynistic, antisemitic, self-confessed bigamist from Kazakhstan, a country with a predominantly Muslim population, clearly plays into numerous stereotypes. Baron Cohen has tried to suggest his character is not, in fact, explicitly Muslim but he is certainly culturally coded as such. And in publicity shots for 2020's *Borat Subsequent Moviefilm*,

Baron Cohen in character is clearly wearing a ring inscribed with the word 'Allah'.

Borat followed in the footsteps of Ali G, a racially ambiguous character who thought he was black but whose name and manner suggested he was an Asian rudeboy from Staines. Then there was Baron Cohen's character in *The Dictator*, Admiral-General Haffaz Aladeen, a misogynist, antisemitic, human rights abusing, dim Muslim leader. Three characters and it starts to look like a pattern.

Lee Kern, a writer and comedian, was part of Baron Cohen's writing team for the Borat sequel. In 2023, during the Israel-Gaza war, he was called out for particularly vile tweets including 'Palestinians are not victims; they are the genocidal perpetrators of racist violence. They cry like little bitches as part of their psychopathic campaign against Jews'. And 'You can fuck off if you try to pretend anything in Israel is even remotely like the sociopathic brainwashing of children that happens below in the reactionary Muslim world. This moronic racist culture is the entire cause of the conflict, and you all know it'.

Kern does not appear to have suffered any professional consequences for his tweets.

Much like broadcaster Julia Hartley-Brewer, who in response to the incel attack on women by Joel Cauchi in a shopping mall in Sydney in April 2024 tweeted 'another day, another terror attack by another Islamic terrorist'. The tweet, posted before the identity of the attacker was known, was viewed more than nine million times before it was deleted. Rachel Riley, a presenter on *Countdown*, had a similar kneejerk response, baselessly linking the attack to support for Palestine. She too had to delete her tweet. Both continue in their presenting roles.

Anti Muslim comments don't carry consequences because Muslims Don't Matter.

Years of dehumanising Muslims leads us to turning a blind eye when Muslims or those perceived to be Muslim are, at one end of the spectrum, discriminated against and at the extreme end maimed and murdered.

Britain's historic relationship with Islam and Muslims is woven through some of our most iconic works of literature. Shakespeare makes dozens of references to Islam in *The Merchant of Venice* and *Othello*. There is even an allusion to the Prophet Mohammed in *Henry VI, Part One* when a character asks, 'Was Mahomet inspired by a dove?' This cites the myth that the Prophet put pieces of corn in his ear to attract a holy dove's inspiration – meaning he was a fraudulent Prophet.

In Chaucer's *Canterbury Tales*, written a hundred years after the Crusades, the 'Doctor of Phisyk' draws on the rich knowledge of the Muslim medieval intellectuals 'Razis, Avicen and Averrois' – otherwise known as Al-Razi, Ibn Sina and Ibn Rushd. But just as Chaucer was guilty of anti-semitism in 'The Prioress's Tale', in which a Christian boy is murdered by Jews, so he is not innocent of anti-Muslim hostility either. In 'The Man of Law's Tale', his main villain is the evil mother of the sultan, who tries to force the heroine Custance to convert to Islam.

Islamophobia, like antisemitism, has deep roots and over the centuries has manifested in different forms.

Orientalism has peppered our literature, art and writings, framing contemporary Western tropes about the East and particularly the Muslim world and Islam. This ideology of imperialism, defined as the exercise of Western power as a civilising force upon an Eastern world that is inferior, underdeveloped and alien, continues to shape both our culture and worryingly foreign and domestic policymaking.

The Palestinian American critic Edward Said, the author of the classic *Orientalism*, wrote in 1980 that 'I have not been able to discover any period in European or American history since the Middle Ages in which Islam was generally discussed or thought about *outside* a framework created by passion, prejudice and political interests.'

In the days following the August 2006 transatlantic aircraft terrorist plot, Martin Amis gave an interview to *The Times*. Amis, a novelist who was knighted shortly before his death in 2023, was quoted as saying: 'What can we do to raise the price of them doing this? There's a definite urge – don't you have it? To say the Muslim community will have to suffer until it gets its house in order. What sort of suffering? Not letting them travel. Deportation, further down the road. Curtailing of freedoms. Strip searching people who look like they're from the Middle East or from Pakistan . . . discriminatory stuff until it hurts the whole community, and they start getting tough with their children . . . it's a huge dereliction on their part.'

In case we think that he merely got carried away in an interview, he wrote similar sentiments in a September 2006 essay, 'The age of horrorism': '[T]he impulse towards rational inquiry is by now very weak in the rank and file of the Muslim male.'

It should disturb us to see a respected novelist call for the persecution and collective punishment of a community, and the stereotyping and stigmatising of all Muslim men – men like my father, my husband and my son.

Responding to Amis, the novelist Pankaj Mishra wrote that his essay's 'pseudo-scholarship and fanatical conviction of moral superiority make it resemble nothing more than one of bin Laden's desperately literary screeds'.

The following year, Chris Morris, the satirist who would later direct the terrorist comedy *Four Lions*, wrote that Amis 'nurtures in his audience a corrosive prejudice against people they've never bothered to meet'. Morris warns of the phenomenon I have often called 'respectable' racism, arguing: 'With ignorance on his side Amis can stare east through the salon window and convince us of a single advancing horde. He is clever. He might put it brilliantly [. . .] But when he speaks, think "[Abu] Hamza".'

That Amis, as well as his close friend Christopher Hitchens, could skew the discourse not from a right-wing perspective but from a supposed liberal left position shows that anti-Muslim racism is found across the political spectrum. But I would argue that while the overt right-wing Islamophobe is far easier to see and challenge, the 'thinking person's Islamophobe' is far more insidious. They sow the seeds of division deep into liberal society, poisoning the very spaces where the calls for anti-racism would normally be heard.

A month after the 7 July 2005 attacks, the novelist Howard Jacobson, who went on to win the Booker Prize in 2010, wrote a column in the *Independent* commenting on Muslims objecting to being stopped and searched. He observed that this 'sounded like a threat' and asked if extremism was the next step: 'If a person feels he has been stopped and searched just once too often is it a natural step for him to blow up a train?' It may have been hyperbole when Jacobson asserted 'It makes you violent, thinking in the language of the popular press', but this approach of targeting based on racial profiling, not solid intelligence, had led to the killing of Brazilian electrician Jean Charles de Menezes on the tube three weeks earlier, when police suspected him of being a suicide bomber.

Jacobson has also spoken about Muslim antisemitism and about why more is not done to challenge it. Antisemitism exists in all communities – Muslims, like Christians and others, are not immune from this form of racism. But what is surprising is that Jacobson's concern about Muslim antisemitism contains little reflection on his own words in shaping the public discourse about Muslims.

In February 2024, he appeared on *Newsnight* to discuss the Gaza bombardment. At the time, thousands of Palestinian civilians had already been killed. Jacobson argued against the BBC showing images of dead Palestinians, images he referred to as 'the same image as it were, or another version of it' because it created 'antisemites', and 'once you're an antisemite, you're an antisemite for life'

It was an indication of how liberal, racially aware and intellectually sensitive people can take their logic to a dehumanising place because in our country Muslims Don't Matter.

Novelist Lionel Shriver, one-time columnist for the *Guardian*, went on *Question Time* in 2019 and defended Boris Johnson's newspaper column comparing women who wear face coverings to 'letter boxes'. She asked a young woman in a hijab who was in the audience why she was so insulted by such a 'light-hearted' remark.

The young woman talked about her everyday experience of being abused on the street, including being told to go back to her 'own country'. She asked Shriver to stop treating offensive comments as a joke. 'I get attacked just for going to the gym,' she said.

Interestingly, in 2021 Shriver argued against migration into the UK, stating that 'the native-born are effectively surrendering their territory without a shot fired'. An odd argument from an American who lived for many years in in the UK and now lives in Portugal. Muslims judged by Shriver to a different standard to the one by which Shriver measures herself.

The acclaimed French author Michel Houellebecq published a novel in 2015 called *Submission*, which imagined a France taken over by conservative Muslims. It became a bestseller, lauded as a daring work among European and UK critics. But although posing as a clever satire, the novel simply perpetuates long-held stereotypes and tropes of what a French president of the Muslim faith would behave like: promoting conversions, ending gender equality, legalising polygamy and forming alliances with Muslim states across the globe. It played into the worst prejudices of French society in a way that fanned the flames of the far right. (Houellebecq, incidentally, had over a decade earlier been acquitted by a French court of inciting racism by calling Islam the 'stupidest religion'.)

Submission feeds into European fears of an Islamic take-over – the anti-Muslim conspiracy theory that warns of a coming 'Eurabia', which has been promoted and popularised by many including the columnist Melanie Phillips and has been the subject of much far-right discussion and political campaigning across Europe.

Submission became a bestseller against the backdrop of the ISIS-inspired attacks on *Charlie Hebdo* in January 2015, targeting cartoonists at the magazine, which had published what many regarded as offensive drawings of the Prophet Mohammed. Appalling as those killings were, the cartoons themselves and those published by the Danish newspaper *Jyllands-Posten* in 2005, drew on a longer context of European anti-Islamic prejudice, which has often been focused through the figure of the Prophet.

The practice of depicting the Prophet Mohammed as a fraudulent character, and as a measure of the falseness of Islam versus the truth of Christianity, has a long history in Europe. Dante might have praised the good pagans Avicenna and Averroes, but he devises a horrible punishment in Hell

for the Prophet in his *Divine Comedy*: the Prophet is repeatedly split from head to toe to symbolise how he 'split'
the Church. (Dante regarded Islam as a form of Christian
heresy.) A church in Bologna still has a fifteenth-century
fresco of the Prophet being 'split', and a seventeenth-century
statue in a Belgian church shows the Prophet being crushed
by angels.

In John Lydgate's fifteenth-century poem *The Fall of
Princes*, the 'false Machomeete' is 'deuoured among swyn',
much like the antisemitic medieval imagery involving Jews
and pigs – the notorious Judensau. Islamophobia in Europe
has often historically overlapped with antisemitism in the
European imagination.

Much of this historical anti-Muslim prejudice was against
the backdrop of a vast and powerful Ottoman Empire, a
major military power that by the seventeenth century had
reached the gates of Vienna. Aside from religious differ-
ences, European Christians felt threatened by the powerful
Muslim other, and rhetorically attacked through the figure
of the Prophet. Mocking Mohammed was a precursor to
viewing his followers as subhuman and Islam as a false faith.

Matthew Dimmock, an academic at the University of
Sussex, has written on how the Prophet was historically rep-
resented on the stage, from Marlowe's *Tamburlaine* from the
late 1580s, through Robert Greene's *Alphonsus* and William
Percy's *Mahomet and his Heaven* to perhaps the most popular,
Voltaire's *Mohammet*.

In France, Voltaire's play was banned in 1742 after only
three performances due to protests by Catholic clergy who

objected to its satirical depiction of the Catholic Church. An Ottoman ambassador visiting Paris also formally protested against the play. Islam was used by Voltaire to critique domestic religion and yet ironically it unified Muslims and Catholics against him.

However, when staged in London it became a huge hit and the English translation went on to be performed 'on London stages in every decade that remained of the eighteenth century, often through two or three seasons, with over twelve different productions', writes Dimmock.

He notes, however, that in 1890 there were strenuous objections to the staging of Henri de Borner's *Mahomet*, which had already been banned in France. Raffiuddin Ahmad, vice-president of the Liverpool Moslem Association, said in a letter to *The Times* that 'The Indian Mussulmans are deeply irritated to learn of the proposed mockery of the Prophet on the stage of a country which has pledged itself to respect their religious feelings, and the Queen of which has been destined by Providence to reign over a greater number of Moslems than any single ruler, Mahomedan or Christian, on the surface of the globe.' He went on to ask, 'Is it right and proper to hurt the religious feelings of so many of your fellow-subjects in the East, to satisfy the whims or fill the coffers of a theatrical company, however influential it may be?'

The Lord Chamberlain's Office intervened, with the head of the department writing 'pray assure all of whom it may concern [. . .] I shall never dream of submitting to you, for the [Lord Chamberlain's] licence, any piece calculated to offend the religious feelings of any portion of Her Majesty's subjects of whatever creed'. The play was not staged.

This was an early example of how the responsibilities of Empire and Britain's Muslim subjects shaped the depiction of Islam and Muslims.

Britain recognised the importance of peace in its territories and the need to acknowledge the religious sensibilities of all those it ruled over, including the small but growing Muslim community in the UK. It moved from an approach where Islam was fair game to a more considered, pragmatic response.

As well as being a fascinating precursor to the Rushdie affair of the late 1980s, this reflects the different approaches Britain has adopted in the past. All sides of this debate should remember this history when navigating today's even more interconnected world, with even more integrated living between different faiths in the UK. If we could show sensitivities during the more brutal era of colonialism, why are we not able to now?

Understanding our history rings true in sport, too. In 2022, Qatar hosted the FIFA World Cup. It was the first time a Muslim nation had done so, and Qatar used the moment to show the best of Islam and Muslim and Arab society, from its family-friendly events to its generous hospitality. Nearly 3.4 million spectators from around the world flocked to this tiny nation.

Yet the furore that led up to the tournament was orientalism in full view: from unproven allegations of corruption and dishonesty to a focus on important but historic human rights abuses; from questioning whether nations such as Qatar had a culture of sport to a spotlight on illiberalism on women's and LGBTQ+ rights.

Qatar rightly introduced workplace reforms and reassured fans that conservative religious sensibilities would not prevent the nation welcoming all, whatever their sexuality. I spoke to a friend who is Muslim and gay, and who lived and worked in Qatar, who told me that officials did not interfere with personal lives unless displays of affection were made in public. But in his experience the response by the authorities was the same for heterosexual couples too. As a lifelong gay rights campaigner, he was appalled at what he saw as the Islamophobic weaponisation of gay rights.

Misleading headlines employed Islamophobic tropes, depicting Muslims as misogynists and callous dictators – a French magazine even published a cartoon depicting the Qatari national team as terrorists. The media meltdown at the winning captain, Argentina's Lionel Messi, being offered a bisht, a traditional robe worn across the Arab world on prestigious occasions and a symbol of honour, by the Emir of Qatar was astonishing to watch. This respectful gesture was denigrated in a *Telegraph* headline as 'The bizarre act that ruined the greatest moment in World Cup history'. The stupidity of the headline was, I presume, apparent on reflection and subsequently changed.

Much was done to malign and undermine the tournament, with the BBC relegating the inclusive and moving opening ceremony starring Morgan Freeman to online viewing only.

What surprised me about this furore was not that we shouldn't be concerned about potential human rights abuses in Qatar, but why we were so *selectively* concerned. Why we hadn't had similar outbursts about other major sporting events in non-Muslim nations such as Russia, which hosted the previous World Cup in 2018, or China, where one million Uighurs and other Muslim minorities are being held in internment camps? The BBC had no qualms about airing the opening ceremony of the 2022 Winter Olympics in Beijing.

In a lengthy press conference, FIFA president Gianni Infantino refuted the criticism of the tournament and of Qatar, denouncing it as rooted in hypocrisy and racism. Infantino may not be everyone's cup of tea but on this he was correct.

(The double standards and hypocrisy are on full display today, as calls for FIFA to exclude Israel, a country before the International Court of Justice on allegations of genocide, are nowhere near the same heightened levels of hysteria among our politicians or in the media.)

English football fans discovered a safe, welcoming and violence-free tournament in Qatar, not least because of the restrictions on alcohol, led one to tell the BBC, 'We're having a lovely time [. . .] our neighbours are Moroccan, Brazilian and Argentinian. Everyone's getting on and sharing things and having time around the pool together [. . .] Everyone's having a great time.' A reflection of both the positive and negatives of a Muslim nation hosting the World Cup would have been more balanced, rather than an obsessive focus on just the problems.

Just as the beautiful game has been an arena for Islamophobia, so has the so-called gentleman's sport.

Cricket has been an integral part of my life. The 1992 England v Pakistan Cricket World Cup final in Melbourne, which Pakistan won, was a gripping experience that remains a defining moment for many British Pakistanis. It inspired generations to take up the sport and British Muslims have played at the highest level.

But in 2020 the rot of racism and particularly Islamophobia in cricket hit the headlines. Sadly, my home county was in the dock.

Azeem Rafiq played professionally for Yorkshire County Cricket Club for eight years. He became the youngest man to captain a Yorkshire side and had captained both the Under-15 and Under-19 England teams. To an outside observer he seemed to be having a perfect career.

But the reality was very different. In November 2021, he appeared before the Culture, Media and Sport Select Committee and gave a horrifying account of the years of abuse and racism he had been subjected to while playing. This included being called a Paki and being pinned down and having alcohol forced down his throat at the age of fifteen by a fellow cricketer. He broke down in tears as he recounted the abuse he and other Asian players had endured, including being called 'bombers' and 'elephant washers', and being told to sit 'near the toilets'.

Some of the most senior players in English cricket stood accused, including Matthew Hoggard and Gary Ballance.

An initial report by Yorkshire in 2021 had found that

'Headingley is less welcoming to Muslim supporters than supporters of other religions, that in some instances, there has been a hostile or intimidating environment for Muslim spectators and that the Club has not taken sufficient action or steps to address this issue.' Only a summary of the report's findings was ever published, and its findings only came to light because of a subsequent ECB report.

The initial report also, bizarrely, labelled the use of the term Paki simply 'banter', and YCCC concluded the abuse to be simply 'inappropriate behaviour'. Subsequent reports, though, concluded that Rafiq had been subjected to serious racism and Islamophobia.

YCCC finally admitted some of the allegations of racism four years after the initial complaints were made, and it took a further two years for the ECB to bring forward disciplinary action.

But what became clear during the subsequent fallout was that the anti-Muslim racism faced by Rafiq was simply the tip of the iceberg.

Muslim players came forward with horrific stories of abuse and bullying, including being urinated on, the desecration of prayer mats and racial slurs directed at them and at Muslim spectators and officials. In 2023, the Independent Commission for Equity in Cricket report by Cindy Butts found that 87 per cent of British Pakistanis and British Bangladeshis faced racism in cricket. In 2022 Cricket Scotland was also found to be 'institutionally racist'.

After years of abuse and threats, Rafiq, fearing for his family's safety, left his home in Barnsley, West Yorkshire and moved overseas. Speaking out meant he was forced to implement his Plan B.

Sport has been the arena for some appalling incidents of anti-Muslim racism, but it has also had the opportunity to create better understanding between peoples.

Positive role models such as the England cricketer Moeen Ali have been great ambassadors and have tried to maintain that very English stiff upper lip despite being on the receiving end of much abuse, including being called 'Osama' by an Australian player during an Ashes Test. Moeen, an openly religious Muslim with his distinct long beard, has not shied away from his Muslimness in public.

After England's historic 2019 Cricket World Cup win, the Dublin-born captain Eoin Morgan was asked whether 'the luck of an Irishman' had got them over the line. 'We had Allah with us as well,' he replied, a comment that went viral.

Morgan championed the diversity of background and cultures as a strength of the team including Yorkshire's Adil Rashid as well as Moeen Ali.

Similarly, in football, the Mo Salah effect has been felt beyond Anfield. The Egyptian striker, a hero to the fans, was at one point one of four Muslims in the Liverpool team, alongside Sadio Mané, Naby Keïta and Xherdan Shaqiri. Mané has spoken of how the club adjusted the training schedules and dietary plans of the players during Ramadan to help them feel more welcome.

A 2019 Stanford University study entitled 'Can Exposure

to Celebrities Reduce Prejudice? The Effect of Mohamed Salah on Islamophobic Behaviours and Attitudes' found an 18.9 per cent drop in the number of hate crimes in Merseyside and the number of anti-Muslim tweets posted by the club supporters halved. The researchers posited that 'these results may be driven by increased familiarity with Islam. Our findings indicate that positive exposure to outgroup role models can reveal new information that humanises the out group writ large.'

Salah's performance of a sujood, or prostrating to God, when scoring a goal is a now a familiar ritual. As is the Liverpool fans' chant, 'If he scores another few, then I'll be Muslim too.'

Representation matters. It's a call made by British actor Riz Ahmed in his 2017 Channel 4 Diversity speech at the Houses of Parliament. It inspired the 'Riz Test', launched by Muslim film buffs tired of the stereotypes and Islamophobic tropes gracing our screens. Much like the Bechdel Test, a set of criteria used to measure representation of women in works of fiction, the Riz Test lays out a series of questions. If the film or TV show features at least one character who is identifiably Muslim are they:

1. Talking about, the victim of, or the perpetrator of terrorism?
2. Presented as irrationally angry?
3. Presented as superstitious, culturally backwards or anti-modern?
4. Presented as a threat to a Western way of life?

5. If the character is male, is he presented as misogynistic? If female, is she presented as oppressed by her male counterparts?

We have occasionally got it right. *Citizen Khan* was Adil Ray's BBC 1 sitcom about British Muslims that both represented and projected – it was for insiders and outsiders. It was British Muslims laughing at themselves alongside others laughing with us. It ran for five seasons and acquired a cult following. Both Sadiq Khan, the Mayor of London, and I agreed to cameo appearances alongside community leader Mr Khan from Sparkhill.

More recently Channel 4's *We Are Lady Parts*, a sitcom about an all-female Muslim punk band, smashes stereotypes of British Muslim women. Written, directed and produced by British Pakistani Nida Manzoor, it certainly passes the Riz Test. It's good to see it come back in 2024 for a second series.

The award-winning independent film *After Love*, written and directed by Aleem Khan, about a white convert to Islam played by Joanna Scanlan is a painful but realistic portrayal of love and betrayal, and shows how difficult issues can be presented to wide audiences.

Monica Ali's novel *Love Marriage* tackles complex relationships and changing identities in multicultural Britain. It feels like a confident insider's narrative, as does Kamila Shamsie's award-winning *Home Fire*, published in 2017, which tackles the various aspects of British Muslim identity and the war on terror.

The novel explores the story of Home Secretary Karamat Lone, a British Pakistani born in a Muslim home who has had to distance himself from his faith to be accepted as British. Seen as someone who is prepared to turn on Muslims for political gain, he strips a British Muslim terrorist of citizenship.

In 2019, life began to imitate art when Sajid Javid, as Home Secretary, stripped Shamima Begum, a British Muslim who was a schoolgirl when she left to join ISIS in 2015, of her British citizenship. As a work of fiction, *Home Fire* was a dramatic portrayal of love, betrayal and competing loyalties; as a decision in government, citizenship-stripping was deeply cynical political posturing, which has perpetuated a grave injustice and is a stain on our country's history.

5

Blind Injustice

The name Shamima Begum has, for some, become synonymous with the challenges the state must confront in its war against terrorism; for others, it is a symptom of how the state has failed British Muslims.

Equally, for some Shamima Begum is a manipulative young woman who was prepared to engage in terrorism with little mercy; for others, she was a vulnerable teenager, groomed by extremists and attracted to an exciting adventure a world away from east London.

Whether she is a perpetrator or a victim (or both), Begum is one of us. Born and raised in Bethnal Green, she had known no other place as home, never lived anywhere but London until she left for Syria in 2015, and only ever held a British passport. To strip her of her citizenship, as the British state did in 2019, to leave her stateless in a prison camp in the Syrian desert, is an injustice that places us on the wrong side of history.

It is against international law to make someone stateless, yet that is exactly what the government has done. Relying on Begum's status as technically eligible for Bangladeshi citizenship – even though she had never visited the country and Bangladesh said it didn't want her – the government revoked Begum's British passport, leaving her in legal limbo.

Treating a fifteen-year-old girl groomed by extremists as an adult, dehumanising a girl who lost three newborn children in as many years, dressed in a headscarf and robes before she swapped them for sleeveless tops and baseball caps in a bid to be accepted by her home country, has been pitiful to watch – and I believe would never have happened had Begum not been Muslim.

The power to strip people of citizenship has existed for 110 years but has been rarely used. It was introduced in the British Nationality and Status of Aliens Act 1914 to allow for the deprivation of citizenship from naturalised citizens who had proven to be 'disaffected or disloyal'.

Enacted shortly after the start of the First World War, it was mostly used to deter British women who lived across the Empire from marrying foreign-born residents or 'aliens'. If they did so marry, they would lose their British nationality. In other words, misogyny and patriarchy were at the heart of this legislation.

Despite two world wars, defending these shores from fascism, the Cold War and the height of the Troubles in Northern Ireland including the period of IRA terrorism

on the British mainland, citizenship-stripping remained a
rarely used power.

From 1949 to 1973, only ten people had their British
citizenship revoked. Between 1973 and 2002, over nearly
thirty years, no one was deprived, even though it was during
this period that the British Nationality Act 1981 was introduced. This allowed for the deprivation of the citizenship
of a naturalised British citizen on the grounds of fraud or
something 'seriously prejudicial to the vital interests of the
United Kingdom', provided that this would not render them
stateless.

Modern nationality law starts with the British Nationality
Act 1981. Its purpose was to register those who were British
and to make clear their entitlement to citizenship. For all
its shortcomings, the Act was an attempt to regularise and
bring into the system through formal paperwork those who
were already British. Let me repeat: *those who were by right
British*. The state was formalising a right that already existed,
not bestowing a new privilege.

Indeed, at the time the Home Office put out leaflets and
disseminated information in communities stressing that
they were merely confirming a right and that nothing in
citizens' status would change. Many were told they didn't
need to exercise this right immediately because the Home
Office, fearing the administrative workload, did not want
to be overwhelmed with applications.

But what was undisputed was their rights. The then
Conservative Home Secretary William Whitelaw clearly
expressed this in the Parliamentary debates on the Bill that

became the Act. He spoke of 'registration as an entitlement' and said that 'decisions taken by the Secretary of State on such applications are not discretionary. If satisfied that the entitlement exists, the Secretary of State must grant the application.'

However, what followed, with subsequent changes to nationality law and an increasingly hostile approach by successive Home Secretaries, was the appalling circumstances exposed in 2018 when members of the Windrush generation – Caribbean people living in the UK who were by right British – were treated like outsiders, foreigners and aliens – and sent back to countries that many of them hadn't been to in decades.

Our hostility to immigrants and immigration created a situation in which we abandoned our own, who were by right British even if they hadn't formally exercised that right by obtaining a passport.

So, the notion of citizenship being a privilege per se seems to be a popular but sadly ignorant and recent mantra. Of course, immigration is not a right – no one has the right to come to this country, nor to be given citizenship upon arrival – but immigration controls are very distinct from nationality rights.

Those who confuse the two do so because their understanding of who is British does not see beyond the colour of someone's skin.

Let me personalise it. A century ago, my family were citizens of the UK and its colonies; they had some rights. All those in the Empire and the Commonwealth did.

When my grandfathers fought for the British Indian Army as British subjects; when they were prepared to give their lives for king and country they did so as citizens. When South Asians took up gruelling jobs in the mills and foundries of Yorkshire, as my grandfather did, he fulfilled his responsibility as a citizen. With that responsibility came rights: the right to be an equal and permanent member of this country – an equal and permanent citizen.

It wasn't a conditional right, or a temporary right or a right we would try to remove in ever more ingenious ways. And it certainly wasn't a privilege: it was earned with strife and blood and sweat and even with life. By taking a British passport, they were formalising a right – not being bestowed a privilege.

Sadly, the othering of our fellow citizens, this chipping away at that basic right of citizenship, ultimately led to the Shamima Begum decision.

All political parties have been a part of the problem. Each has over time torn down that basic belief that all citizens and citizenships in this country are and should be equal, and that as a citizen you are a permanent member, that to possess British citizenship is to possess a fundamental right, including the right of abode.

Courts recognised this fundamental right, including the High Court in the case of D4 and the Court of Appeal in Pham v Home Secretary, a case on the citizenship deprivation of P, a British citizen born in Vietnam but convicted of terrorism offences and incarcerated in the United States. The judgment said: 'The right to nationality is an important and weighty right. It is properly described as the right to have other rights, such as the right to reside in the country of residence and to consular protection and so on.'

We should all be appalled that, decades on from the British Nationality Act 1981, our country is telling my children and their children that they are second-class citizens. That their nationality is a privilege, that it's conditional and can be taken away. This is the shocking real-life consequence of years of incremental legislation.

In 2022 the issue was once more before Parliament, this time because the government lost in the Court of Appeal, when the court decided that citizenship had been unlawfully stripped when it had been done so without giving notice.

In another sleight of hand, the government not only wanted to strip citizenship but wanted to do so without giving any notice and in secret. As Maya Foa, the director of Reprieve, a legal and human rights organisation, said, 'a person accused of speeding would be afforded more rights than someone at risk of being deprived of their British nationality'.

The recent years of Conservative government were some of the worst for citizenship deprivation. The Home Office is not transparent on how many orders were made and why, but from what has managed to find its way into the public domain, more than a thousand orders for deprivation were made between 2010 and 2022, and in 2017 alone there were over a hundred cases. Of these, 217 orders were for 'the public good'.

In the last twenty years our citizenship-stripping has

escalated and expanded beyond anything previous generations could have imagined.

Laws that lay dormant for most of the past century have,
starting in the Blair New Labour years, been used to create a
climate that was described by former Tory MP Jacob Rees-
Mogg (of all people) as 'a fundamentally racist policy' that
creates 'two categories of Briton' and 'denies the absolute
Britishness of all those who are either recent immigrants
themselves or their children'.

We were reluctant to strip someone of their citizenship
when we were an overwhelmingly white nation, but the
more diverse we have become the more eager we have been
to use this provision. Uncomfortable as it may be, this is
a fact.

A hardly used piece of legislation morphed into a catch-
all law that now covers around 40 per cent of our ethnic
minority communities.

That change took place through the attempt to remove
one man from UK shores. Abu Hamza al-Masri, born in
Egypt, immigrated to the UK in 1979 to study engineering.
Later he married a local girl and became a British citizen.
In 2012, he was extradited to the United States on terrorism charges and is currently serving a life sentence without
parole in Colorado. Back in the 1990s, he became a hate
figure, a tabloid clown and a symbol of the scary Muslim
other, seen as both a welfare scrounger and the enemy
within.

From the way he dressed to his fiery speeches at Finsbury
Park Mosque, where he was the imam, from his robes and

caps to his distinct prosthetic hook and eye patch, he was all things foreign and scary. As Bonnie Honig says in her essay 'A Legacy of Xenophobia', 'although we may [. . .] sometimes persecute people because they are foreign, the deeper truth is that we almost always make foreign whom we persecute'.

This made the 2002 law change, often described as the Abu Hamza amendment, pass without much controversy. For the first time, citizens born British could be stripped of their citizenship. It also introduced the much broader category of anything 'seriously prejudicial to the vital interests of the United Kingdom', a test which was extended in 2006 to simply 'conducive to the public good'.

Abu Hamza was as despised among Britain's Muslims as he was by the mainstream. The most popular conspiracy theory was that he was working for British intelligence, a deliberate provocateur placed at the heart of the community to cause unrest and division. No one was sad to see him go when he was extradited to the US, but the fallout of successive attempts to remove him continues to blight the lives of British Muslims.

We are not talking about newly arriving immigrants: we are talking about our fellow British citizens. If your forefathers fought for this country as part of the Commonwealth, as mine did, and came here when Britain needed a workforce, as mine did, and you have a family history of over half a century on these shores, as mine do, it includes you as it includes me.

If you are Jewish and thus entitled to Israeli citizenship under Israel's 'right of return', it includes you; if you are

South Asian and the country your forefathers were born in extends to you the right to apply for citizenship, whether you take up that offer or not, it includes you. It includes Members of Parliament, members of our armed forces and their families. This shocking state should disturb all right-thinking people.

The law has created different classes of citizenship, as again Rees-Mogg has noted: 'Those with no right to another nationality are in the first-class carriage', while 'those who themselves came to the UK or whose parents did so are in the second-class carriage'.

What started with Abu Hamza was stepped up post-7/7 and again during the ISIS years, and eventually led to young British women being stranded stateless in the deserts of the Middle East.

A petition to revoke the citizenship of those who went abroad to join ISIS received the highest number of signatures to any petition in the last Parliament (580,000). Many of our democratically engaged fellow citizens also support citizenship deprivation. Populist tabloid columnists will argue that if you commit a serious crime then you should lose your citizenship.

That argument baffles me.

If we want to make citizenship-stripping a punishment for a crime, then surely it must apply to all who engage in such crimes, not some. The rule of law and equality before the law is an oft-cited British value, so whether your crime is terrorism, fraud or a sexual offence, why should punishment depend on ancestry or heritage?

If two young people, both British nationals, commit the same offence, why does the law allow for one to be permanently removed from the country while the other remains a Brit?

Shamima Begum and others like her are *our* problem. She was shaped and formed in our country; it's what made her who she is. She was identified as 'at risk' by her school months before she left, noting that 'she may leave home and school' and there was a 'chance she may go to Syria'.

The police spoke to her weeks before she left, choosing to inform her parents via a letter they handed to her, which was never received by the family. It has subsequently been alleged by filmmaker and journalist Richard Kerbaj that the person who helped facilitate Begum's travel to Syria was working with Canadian intelligence as a double agent. Murky indeed.

Clearly, many failed her, but even if she is an unquestionable criminal she should be charged, tried and convicted under our laws and serve in our prisons. If citizenship-stripping is about protecting our country from terrorism, then leaving stateless young men and women to roam lawless around the world does precisely the opposite.

Post the ISIS era, the most dangerous fighters – around 360 of them – have made their way back to these shores. Many have faced no sanction or punishment. Women and young children remained stranded; we chose to make an example of them. We picked on the easy targets.

What made the Begum decision particularly distasteful was that the Home Secretary made the order in 2019, when

Shamima Begum was nineteen. Sajid Javid was only able to make the decision because she was under the age of twenty-one and according to Bangladeshi law her entitlement to exercise the option to obtain Bangladeshi citizenship was only possible up to that age, at which point, if not exercised, it lapsed. The fact that Begum had an option that she had not exercised nor shown any intention of exercising, and had not even visited Bangladesh, was simply irrelevant when Javid determined that her presence was not 'conducive to public good'.

The fact that Bangladesh within days made clear that Begum was not a Bangladeshi citizen and there was 'no question' of her even being allowed into the country means Begum has been stripped based upon an option she did not exercise and which, had she done, would not have been offered.

Javid relied upon the catch-all 'conducive to public good' as well as vague national security concerns as carte blanche to do as he pleased. It has meant that her subsequent appeals have not been successful because the only decision the courts can rule on is whether the decision was unlawful – not whether it was unfair, unprincipled, unscrupulous and unjust.

It seems British politicians have a very liberal approach to being authoritarian. Bobbie Mills, in a blog post for the European Network on Statelessness, has warned: 'Not only does Britain have the most developed legal deprivation powers among liberal democracies, it has also applied these powers much more liberally.'

*

I grew up in a household where my parents were paranoid about keeping all their paperwork safe in a Hitachi case. Windrush proved they were right, when many a settled British person had to prove their right to be here decades after they arrived. What the Begum case has shown, though, is that however well documented, many British Muslims are only as British as the latest legislation allows. That our children and grandchildren must forever be the 'good immigrant' in case we outstay our welcome. That however hard we try we still don't belong; we don't matter.

As novelist and critic Philip Hensher eloquently wrote of the Abu Hamza case in 2003, 'He will be subject to punishment beyond that imposed on most British citizens; his rights of free speech will be more circumscribed. He may not, as Englishmen have done for centuries, say that things would be greatly improved if someone blew up Parliament. He must watch his step.'

Europe, the US and Canada followed our lead in disowning its citizens who joined ISIS. A decade on, they have seen the error of their ways with France, Germany, Sweden, the US, Canada and others now taking back and rehabilitating their citizens, particularly women and children. We remain out of step with our allies and out of step with our own historic approach.

Politicians like Javid and Braverman often project themselves as patriots, as people fighting to preserve tradition, culture and heritage. Yet by waging culture wars they destroy the values we should be defending. When we fundamentally undermine long-standing values and norms in our society, we are damaging our country.

Take the issue of natural justice, the age-old rules and conventions that define procedural fairness, the principles that protect our rights as individuals to fair treatment in legal proceedings. They are an essential component of the rule of law. One of the Latin maxims I learnt as a young lawyer and can still recall decades later, *Audi alteram partem* (let the other party be heard), includes the right to be informed of the allegations against you. And yet in the UK we now have a system of secret justice where the evidence against an individual is neither disclosed to them nor their representatives; where 'special advocates' have access to evidence but no access to the accused; where decisions can be made to effectively banish you from the place you were born and have lived your entire life; and where Muslims are its primary victims.

The Special Immigration Appeals Commission and its use of closed material proceedings are a widely used and yet little-known aspect of our legal system. Concerns about the process are well documented in a report entitled 'Secret Justice' written by the legal charity JUSTICE. Among other issues, the report gave examples of the same piece of secret evidence being used to make contradictory cases in different proceedings behind closed doors. This only came to light because the special advocate, the lawyer assigned by the government to have access to the 'secret evidence', coincidentally happened to be involved in both cases and raised the alarm.

Let me be clear. As a lawyer and a Privy Councillor, I accept that emergency situations and matters of national security require us – in exceptional circumstances – to sidestep rules of natural justice. I am also clear that these moments need to be genuinely exceptional and exercised with the utmost care and attention, and have comprehensive and robust oversight.

I was a minister in the government that passed the Justice and Security Act 2013, which both extended the use of secret justice but also agreed to review these closed material proceedings within five years of the passing of the Act. That deadline to review expired in 2018. The government, after much foot-dragging, eventually appointed a reviewer in 2021. Sir Duncan Ouseley, a retired High Court judge, submitted his report in December 2022. The government failed to respond to the review until the dying days of the last Conservative government. On 29 May 2024, the day before the dissolution of Parliament, the response was published, rejecting important recommendations including a collective submission by special advocates that would have ensured that when we step away from our values we do so with the utmost care.

As in most areas that impact British Muslims, there has been little political will to review, rethink and reset. Instead, mission creep has set in, generating a parallel system of secret injustice.

British values are defined by government as democracy, the rule of law, individual liberty and mutual respect and tolerance for those of different faiths and beliefs. Values we have seen many members of successive governments neither live by nor promote. Yet these values are supposed to underpin a policy known as Prevent.

Prevent is one of four parts of the Contest counter-terrorism strategy; the other three are Protect, Prepare and Pursue. Prevent's stated aim is to 'stop people becoming terrorists or supporting terrorism'. It was introduced in 2006 to tackle disadvantage, inequalities and discrimination. It was intended as a support mechanism, a safeguarding measure led by communities impacted by terrorism. It acknowledged that Islamophobia, racism and inequality of opportunity fed terrorism. It was about creating an environment in which ideas could be debated, and communities were encouraged to engage in civic challenge. It was, in effect, a battle of ideas.

It was supposed to be a helpful upstream intervention to stop ideas being turned into violence – and yet Prevent has become one of the most toxic and politicised policies among British Muslims, the community it overwhelmingly targets.

In 2015, in the final months of the coalition government, Michael Gove succeeded in placing Prevent on a statutory footing through the Counter-Terrorism and Security Act 2015. This transformed this toxic and by now failing policy into one that put an obligation on public sector bodies and institutions such as schools and the NHS to effectively act as a surveillance and reporting system for all things 'extremist'.

The justification for this was the so-called Trojan Horse scandal in Birmingham's schools. The affair is almost impossible to explain in a few paragraphs. It has been the subject of an eight-part *New York Times* podcast and numerous government and academic reports – and yet remains mysterious.

In 2013, an anonymous letter appeared on a Labour councillor's desk in Birmingham. The letter turned out to be a hoax but its contents, alleging an attempt by 'Islamist' parents, teachers and governors to take over local schools, reshaped counter-terrorism policy and the state's relationship with British Muslims.

The letter's author has not been identified; the allegations were false, and both a local authority and a separate government-commissioned report found no evidence of terrorism. Although the government-commissioned report purported to show 'co-ordinated, deliberate and sustained action' by Muslim teachers to 'introduce an intolerant and aggressive Islamic ethos', the subsequent cases against teachers at the respective schools failed spectacularly. The framing of the issue by media and politicians as an 'extremist plot' couldn't be further from the truth. Academics who have rigorously analysed the chain of events that sparked the storm have rightly concluded that a public inquiry is needed to get the facts right and overturn miscarriages of justice.

But the Trojan Horse affair provided a convenient moment for Gove, then Secretary of State for Education, and his political adviser Dominic Cummings, later Boris Johnson's adviser, to initiate a course of action that resulted in placing Prevent on a statutory footing. That meant that an army of public sectors workers, with little or no training, little transparency and no outside scrutiny of their activities, were expected to assess and determine indicators of radicalisation.

This resulted in thousands of referrals: 12,984 to the year ending March 2024, of which over 90 per cent turned out to have little or no basis. It left a community feeling under siege. The smallest misunderstanding or the personal prejudices of a teacher had the potential to ruin lives – and many lives have been.

Take the Lancashire dinner lady whose colleagues took exception to her enforcing rules to keep separate utensils for halal and non-halal meal preparation in the school kitchen. She was 'set up' under false allegations that she 'supported ISIS', resulting in her suspension and a disciplinary hearing. An appeal panel reversed her suspension but so bad was the impact on her health, she has been unable to return to work. Or the four-year-old boy whose mother was told he had been referred to Prevent by his nursery for pronouncing cucumber as 'cooker bomb'.

Or the Muslim teenager from Birmingham referred to Prevent by his college when he took to wearing traditional Arab dress. So certain were the authorities that his changed behaviour was a sign of 'radicalisation' that when he visited Calais to assist refugees, police assumed he had fled to Syria. As his lawyer put it, 'If he was dressed in black and wearing eyeliner, they wouldn't have gone after him. Muslim kids are not afforded the same opportunity of rebelling as white kids are.'

The Prevent duty was what we now call 'cancel culture'. It created a chilling effect, pushing Muslims out of the public domain for fear of being tarnished as extremist. It strangled the organic growth of Muslim civil society, a development I and many like me had encouraged, and it cemented the government's guilt-by-association approach, which used tenuous links with people with apparently extreme views to exclude British Muslims from public life.

Universities also contributed to risk-averse strategies by shutting down free speech and healthy debate. More recently, Prevent has been used to police and silence young people wanting to show solidarity with Palestinian children. I have taken call after call from anxious parents fearful of the climate in our educational establishments and the impact it is having on the confidence of their children and their career prospects. British Muslims were the first community in our country to be cancelled by government and they continue to have their right to free speech stifled.

The Trojan Horse scandal enabled Gove to change the course of hostile policymaking regarding British Muslims. It was a strategy he had outlined in some detail in a 2006 book, *Celsius 7/7*, which by bizarre coincidence has a chapter titled 'Trojan Horse'.

Celsius 7/7, described by historian William Dalrymple as a 'confused epic of simplistic incomprehension', was nonetheless treated as a blueprint for government thinking. The Trojan Horse scandal, however much a hoax, provided the necessary trigger for Gove to implement much of what he had intended to do for years.

I initially treated Gove's ramblings as evidence of an obsessive ideology which most of my colleagues in government could see was not rooted in fact or evidence. For example, his belief that 'a sizeable minority of British Muslims hold rejectionist Islamist views', which he compares to Nazism and communism, was simply not supported by experts, including our intelligence services. But over time politics, populism and personal ambition outranked the evidence.

I recall watching up close the political tussle between Gove and Theresa May during the Trojan Horse affair, with May reminding Gove that it was his academy schools reforms that had led to a lack of local oversight, while Gove wanted the May-led Home Office to take the blame. This had become a high-profile political issue and each in their own way had an eye on future leadership ambitions.

The Trojan Horse affair was being managed as a governance issue in both Birmingham City Council and in government until the 'bogus' letter was leaked to the media, unleashing a torrent of inflammatory media coverage.

Gove's appointment of the former deputy assistant commissioner at the Metropolitan Police and head of counter-terrorism Peter Clarke to lead an inquiry into twenty-five Birmingham schools was seen as provocative and confrontational. It was questioned by Birmingham City Council, local Members of Parliament and West Midlands Police. Chris Sims, West Midlands chief constable, called the appointment of Peter Clarke 'desperately unfortunate' and the local Police and Crime Commissioner Bob Jones saw it as an attempt to 'divert attention away from the governance and diversity issues that might be embarrassing to his policies and approach to school governance'.

Interestingly, Clarke said his inquiry found no evidence of extremism but did find that there were 'a number of people, associated with each other and in positions of influence in schools and governing bodies, who espouse, sympathise or fail to challenge extremist views' – a statement that could just as easily be made about the last Conservative government.

Multiple other investigations were instigated, including one by Ian Kershaw commissioned by the local authority, which found 'no evidence of a conspiracy to promote an anti-British agenda, violent extremism or radicalisation'. The leader of Birmingham City Council, Sir Albert Bore, said he did not believe there to be any 'plot'.

A report by the ex-chief inspector of Ofsted, Sir Michael Wilshaw, found various governance failings and the schools were subsequently downgraded. One of the schools implicated was Park View Academy, which in 2012 had been declared an 'outstanding' by Ofsted, and Wilshaw stated that 'all schools should be like this'. Park View Educational Trust described the subsequent inquiry and the imposing of special measures as a 'witch hunt'.

In March 2015 the Education Select Committee criticised a lack of coordination between the various Trojan Horse inquiries and accepted that there was no evidence of a plot. Fifteen teachers and senior staff were the subject of disciplinary proceedings. All bar one collapsed because the Department of Education failed to supply evidence to support the cases against the accused.

The cost to the taxpayer of Gove's folly in pursuing the

disciplinary cases has been over £1 million, costs which the Department of Education tried to withhold from publication but was forced to release after Freedom of Information requests by the BBC and an appeal to the Information Commissioner's Office.

Teachers and senior staff were hounded by the press and politicians while pupils suffered the consequences of disrupted teaching, media sensationalism and the stigma of being associated with a 'suspect' school. Multiple lives ruined, multiple schools decimated, their Ofsted ratings impacted, education damaged, with GCSE results falling from 73 per cent A–C grades to 57 per cent.

The affair continued to shadow the lives of young Muslims. In 2015, Suriyah Bi, an Oxford University graduate, lost her job as a teaching assistant for objecting to a teacher showing eleven-year-olds (some of whom had special needs) YouTube videos of the 9/11 attacks. A safeguarding checklist completed by the school after Bi was sacked detailed that she had been head girl in a school that was subsequently embroiled in the Trojan Horse scandal and that her concerns about the use of the 9/11 footage were because 'it offended her as a Muslim'.

It was subsequently determined by the school, in a senior management meeting, that the 9/11 footage should never have been shown because of its 18 rating. Bi eventually won her case for unfair dismissal.

To date there has been no recourse to justice for the Birmingham teachers; no remedial action for the schools dragged into the glare of negative media coverage; no support for the children who had their education derailed, their names forever associated with an 'extremist' school and their job prospects impacted; no effort at rebuilding confidence in Muslim communities and the schools affected by the government's mishandling; and, crucially, no apology to any of those children harmed.

Gove's obsession with Muslims led to him, in his last ministerial role as Communities Secretary, defunding a programme called Remembering Srebrenica, an initiative to commemorate the Serbian genocide of Bosnian Muslims in 1995 which tackled anti-Muslim hatred and other forms of racism. It was a programme I had started in 2012, supported by David Cameron as PM and William Hague as Foreign Secretary. Against independent civil service advice, Gove revoked all its funding while in the same year increased funding for work to tackle antisemitism through Holocaust remembrance and education. (Months later, some funding was restored after the intervention of senior ex-Cabinet ministers.)

Over the last two decades there have been frightening developments: the expansion of Prevent; the stripping of citizenship; the Special Immigration Appeals Commission; the proliferation of closed material proceedings, where citizens are not given access to the evidence or even the basis of the case against them in court; harassment while passing through border control, which is now just accepted as normal by so many of us; and the most appalling injustices, impacting the outcome of people's lives and livelihoods with no attempt to redress the error or learn from the mistakes.

The hostile climate is overwhelming and the need to change course is urgent.

If we allow this to fester it will in the end infect the whole nation and change who we are for ever. If we want to preserve our values, then that starts with a commitment not to erode them. If we wouldn't inflict these policies on the majority, we should question why they are considered appropriate to impose on a minority. As Martin Luther King, Jr said: 'Injustice anywhere is a threat to justice everywhere.'

6

Unequal Nation

In 2018, giving evidence before the Home Affairs Select Committee on its inquiry into hate crime and its violent consequences, I was asked whether I would like to see more good news stories in the press about Muslims to counterbalance the bad news stories. I said I would settle for accurate news stories.

British Muslims do not need special treatment: they just need equal treatment. The exceptionalising of Muslim communities, the treatment of them in ways we would not treat others, undoubtedly harms Muslims but also harms the rest of us.

To take one example: Islamophobia is bad for business. It damages communities and affects our economies. At a time of increased global investment, when countries and individuals are looking for places to put their wealth, when young people are looking for places to study, when entre-preneurs are looking for welcoming countries and when a trained, skilled and globally mobile workforce is a sought-after resource, how the UK sets out its stall will be shaped by the society we choose to be. The 2024 far-right racist riots and the knock-on effect of countries around the world warning their citizens not to travel to areas of the UK did exactly the opposite.

A 2019 analysis by the Religious Freedom and Business Foundation found that since the 2008 financial crisis, countries with decreasing levels of religious restrictions and hostilities experienced double the rate of GDP growth as those where religious restrictions and hostilities increased. That is to say, there is a positive relationship between reli-gious freedoms and economic growth.

A World Economic Forum opinion column from 2014 cited freedom of religion and belief as one of three factors significantly associated with global economic growth.

Georgetown University and Brigham Young University, in a 2014 study on religious freedom and business, similarly concluded that 'religious freedom contributes to better economic and business outcomes'. The study also found 'innovative strength to be more than twice as likely among countries with low religious restrictions and hostilities and found a positive relationship between religious freedom and ten of the twelve pillars of global competitiveness, as measured by the World Economic Forum's Global Competitiveness Index'.

I have spent decades campaigning against the persecution

of minorities, as an activist, as a lawyer and as a government minister. As the Minister for Human Rights, I designated freedom of religion and/or belief as my key focus, led the drive for greater religious literacy and established our leading international work on challenging the persecution of religious minorities – particularly Christians.

It's an issue I highlighted in a speech at Georgetown University in 2013, in which I warned of the disturbing worldwide rise in religious persecution. I warned of a Christian exodus of 'biblical proportions from parts of the world where Christianity was first born and established'.

Britain can and should be a comfortably multi-religious and tolerant society. As part of that, in 2012 I led the UK's first efforts in issuing an Islamic bond or sukuk. The concept of a sukuk is rooted in the religious belief that usury is forbidden, that the making of money via interest payments is exploitative and thus transactions should be tied to assets.

The amount was small and the offering oversubscribed eleven times over, but the issuance sent a message that Britain was open for Islamic business, a stall first set out by Gordon Brown when he was prime minister. As a major financial centre, London has been a hub for the development of the private Islamic financial sector, and between 2010 and 2014 I was proud to expand this into the public sector too.

In 2013, we became the first non-Muslim country to host the World Islamic Economic Forum and the first to issue a government bond. In 2021, the UK issued its second sukuk.

Trading with a worldwide Muslim population of nearly

two billion, a young community both as a market and a resource, is the right thing to do and in our national interest.

Being a friendly place for Muslims from around the world pays economic dividends – something we recognised in 2010. Sadly, it's a view that fell out of favour in government and instead we got a culture of hostility that is harming our national interest.

It is also in the UK's interest to create a climate where our own Muslims, British Muslims, become an integral and fully utilised part of our economy. The value of the Muslim pound – the cumulative buying power of British Muslims, the rise in Muslim entrepreneurs, the hundreds of thousands of small businesses that form the backbone of community life is enormous. The value of the halal meat and poultry sector alone is approximately £1.7 billion out of an overall total of £11 billion for the UK meat industry.

Big businesses are now chasing the Muslim pound. Next launched its first modest wear collection for women in 2022 and outdoor clothing specialists Trekmates created the first-ever waterproof and windproof hijab and niqab together with Amira Patel, founder of the Wanderlust Women Group. Another outdoor clothing specialist, Berghaus, collaborated with the Scottish Muslim hiker Zahrah Mahmood on designing a hijab suitable for dealing with the elements.

Despite all this positivity, though, the impact of Islamophobia and anti-Muslim racism on the economy is real.

In 2016, the Women and Equalities Parliamentary Committee published a report, 'Employment Opportunities for Muslims in the UK'. It was compiled by a group of cross-party MPs led by Conservative Maria Miller, a former Secretary of State for Culture, Media and Sport, who commented: 'The report underlines the positive contribution of Muslims across the UK, and the urgent need to make equality of opportunity a reality for people of every faith and background.' Muslim women were found to be the most economically disadvantaged group in British society.

Statistics from 2015 suggested that Muslim women are three times more likely to be unemployed than women generally and twice as likely (58 per cent) to be economically inactive compared to all women (27 per cent). Although several reasons were cited, the evidence suggested that a major factor was 'stereotypical views of Muslim women, which may be held by employers or communities, can act as a barrier to employment opportunities'.

Research published by Bristol University in 2015 shows the extent of discrimination faced by Muslim women, noting that they are 71 per cent more likely than white Christian women to be unemployed, even after controlling for factors such as language abilities, education, marital status, number of children and strength of religious belief.

And although the picture seemed to be getting better, with 45 per cent more Muslim women in work in 2016 than they were in 2011, the 'triple penalty' faced by Muslim women (gender, race and religion) makes the issue particularly challenging.

Maria Miller's report contained nineteen recommendations, and it was noted that 'the government needs to directly address workplace discrimination, provide effective support to work, widen access to university, and properly support the aspirations of Muslim women'.

It was also stated that the linking of initiatives on integration to schemes like Prevent (see Chapter 5) had been damaging: 'The report recommends that the Government must work to rebuild trust with Muslim communities by adopting an approach to integration which focuses on how it improves the life chances of disadvantaged communities rather than through the lens of counter-extremism.'

The report concluded that 'inequality, discrimination and Islamophobia particularly affect the lives of Muslim women when looking for work and once they are in work'.

The WEC report recommended that the government should raise awareness among employers of what constitutes illegal discrimination. It also recommended name-blind recruitment and for employers to 'pay particular attention to the impact of discrimination and the fear of discrimination in the workplace for Muslim women who wear cultural or religious dress'.

They heard testimonies from women wearing headscarves who had managed to secure interviews but found, after meeting face to face, the job offer did not materialise. They thought that this 'might be because employers hold stereotypical views of Muslim women, assuming they are likely to need maternity leave, flexible working, be uncommitted, unsocial and so on.' Even if they did secure a job, many women continued to suffer 'negative stereotyping'.

In 2015, Citizens UK established a Citizens Commission

on Islam, Participation and Public Life chaired by the former Attorney General Dominic Grieve. Two years later, they published their report – *The Missing Muslims: Unlocking British Muslim Potential for the Benefit of All* – which found that employment disadvantages and discrimination act as barriers to integration for British Muslims.

The report stated that 'more needs to be done, not just to provide more equitable access to opportunities for British Muslims but to allow the British economy to harness the full potential of this significant section of the population'. Disturbingly, it found that 'discrimination, and fears of being discriminated against, are actively discouraging participation and contributing to disillusionment with the political process among young British Muslims'. A lack of action against those perpetrating anti-Muslim prejudice also led to Muslims feeling disenfranchised.

It recommended ending the stalemate in engagement of Muslim communities (see Chapter 1); for the government to develop an integration strategy and adopt a definition of anti-Muslim prejudice; for the Independent Press Standards Organisation to provide guidance on accurate reporting on Muslim issues; and for employers to sign up to a commitment to name-blind applications, unconscious bias and religious and cultural literacy training, as well as to support mentoring initiatives.

Professor Jacqueline Stevenson's 2017 report on young Muslims and social mobility argues that 'racism and discrimination in the workplace is working to limit aspiration and prevent young Muslims from "aiming high" and fulfilling their potential'. Stevenson also found that despite Muslims being well represented in higher education – higher numbers enter university than other groups – they are under-represented in professional and managerial roles.

She refers to layers of discrimination in higher education, from the application process to campus experience and degree attainment. 'Muslims are excluded, discriminated against, or failed, at all stages of their transition from education to employment.'

Research on the labour market by academics Nabil Khattab and Tariq Modood found that although all non-white groups face a penalty likely to be associated with their skin colour, Muslims faced a greater penalty, with black Muslims facing the highest penalty of all. In the comparison between white groups, only white Muslims faced a substantial penalty.

There seems to be a hierarchy of discrimination highly determined by colour and religion. Among Christians, only black Christians face a significant penalty. All black groups faced a penalty, but black Muslims faced the severest of all.

So, according to Khattab and Modood, 'if you are a Muslim in the United Kingdom, you are likely to face a penalty regardless of your colour or geography. If you are a Christian in the United Kingdom, you are not likely to face any penalties unless you are black. If you are white, you will also be protected unless you are a Muslim.'

One thing is clear: in the labour market, Muslims Don't Matter.

Unfortunately, there has been little take-up of the

recommendations by government. Instead, the response can be summarised as: we care if you're held back because of ethnicity and gender, but not if the reason is religious identity.

In recent years, three moments have stood out for me, where discrimination and prejudice shaped the narrative and highlighted the unequal and unfair treatment of British Muslims.

In 2020, as the Covid pandemic spread, it was striking that some of the early NHS professionals we lost were Muslim.

Dr Adil El Tayar was an organ transplant specialist who had been volunteering in accident and emergency; Dr Habib Zaidi was a general practitioner; and Dr Amged El Hawrani was an ear, nose and throat specialist. All three died saving lives at a time when personal protective equipment wasn't always available. They put the lives of their patients above their own. Days later Areema Nasreen, a Muslim nurse from Walsall, died on a ventilator in the hospital in which she worked.

Their faith put them on the front line. Rather than making them less British, being Muslim made their commitment to humanity, their profession and their country align.

There was a brief moment of soul-searching about their sacrifices, which, like the weekly clapping for carers, was soon forgotten.

It's always fascinated me how, despite the NHS being heavily serviced by Muslim doctors and nurses, Muslims are not generally seen as 'life savers' but rather 'life takers' because of the handful of British Muslims who have committed deadly terrorist acts.

Analysis by the Office for National Statistics found that the 'highest age-standardised mortality rates of deaths involving COVID-19 were in the Muslim religious group'. Before the data was publicly available, I was acutely aware from anecdotal information that the Muslim community was losing many to the coronavirus.

It was therefore galling when far-right rhetoric started to suggest that Britain's Muslims were *responsible* for spreading the virus. The suggestion that Muslims were not following the rules like everyone else was not just a conspiracy theory found in dark corners of social networks. It was repeated by politicians, including my Conservative colleagues.

The Conservative MP for Calder Valley, Craig Whittaker, accused Muslims in West Yorkshire, my home county, of not taking the pandemic seriously, saying the 'vast majority' of those breaking the rules in his constituency were from black and ethnic minority communities, and singling out Muslims.

When asked about Whittaker's comments, Prime Minister Boris Johnson, rather than condemn them, chose to thank the 'mosques and imams who have worked hard with us to get the message across'. Thus subtly implying that Muslims were breaking the rules more than others, even as he and his set were partying in Downing Street.

At the time of these comments, much was already in the public domain about Covid rules being flouted by 'beach lovers, pub goers, illegal ravers, face mask protestors and football cup win celebrators' none of whom, as I highlighted at the time, had been categorised by race or religion.

A report in the *International Journal of Human and Health Sciences* in 2022 reported on the experiences of male Muslim healthcare workers during Covid, including discrimination towards men with beards worn for religious reasons, and the pressure to shave beards because of inadequate PPE.

Such microaggressions were not new. In 2020, the Muslim Doctors Association and Allied Health Professionals had, alongside the Grey Area, presented findings of a survey that found widespread experiences of bias and prejudice: almost 40 per cent of healthcare workers reported having received verbal abuse from colleagues about their faith, more than 60 per cent did not feel comfortable raising concerns at work, 40 per cent had to compromise on practising their faith at work and almost 90 per cent said they did not know Muslims in leadership and management positions. A majority had experienced being othered, stereotyping and threats resulting in them concealing their true selves.

In 2022, the Royal College of General Practitioners published *Islamophobia: Time to Tackle Denial*. This report built on the 2015 King's Fund study that found Muslim healthcare workers were far more likely to experience discrimination in comparison to any other religion.

In 2023 the General Medical Council (GMC), the public body that maintains a register of doctors in the UK, in its report *Tackling Disadvantage in Medical Education*, did an analysis of educational and career outcomes by ethnicity and the interplay with other personal characteristics. Disturbingly, it found that Muslims had the second lowest pass rate for specialty exams and were the religious group most likely to have an unsatisfactory outcome at their annual review on competency progression.

In 2024 the appalling treatment of Muslim healthcare professionals once again reared its ugly head, this time amid Israel's attack on Gaza. As the Palestinian death toll exceeded tens of thousands, the majority women and children, I started receiving calls from Muslim doctors, nurses and other health workers facing an onslaught of complaints and a spike in referrals to the GMC. The GMC's stated duty is to 'protect, promote and maintain the health, safety and wellbeing of the public'. It has the power to sanction medics, including suspending doctors and even permanently banning them from the profession.

Many British doctors working with charities and aid agencies found themselves on the frontline as war broke out. British doctors and healthcare workers organised some of the early vigils outside Downing Street and raised the alarm about the life-threatening situation their colleagues faced in Gaza, including allegations of Israel's deliberate targeting of hospitals and healthcare workers.

They rightly railed against what were clear breaches of the Geneva Convention, which protects 'under all circumstances' healthcare workers including those 'engaged in the collection, transport and treatment of the wounded and the sick and in the administration of medical formations and establishments'.

Far from doctors being off-limits, it seemed like the Israeli army was treating them as targets. Pictures of doctors stripped, bound and blindfolded were seen across the globe. Their profession was under attack, their colleagues were in the firing line and many British Muslims working in the NHS rightly felt the need to speak out and show solidarity. Yet many felt they were being singled out, stifled and silenced.

According to the GMC, 53,459 doctors in the UK identify as Muslim – 17 per cent of all licensed in the UK. The BBC reported that in the four months after the 7 October attack, sixty British medical professionals were reported for alleged antisemitic conduct or remarks made against their colleagues. During the same period, sixteen allegations of Islamophobia were made, up from three in the preceding nine months.

The GMC confirmed that '[s]ince October 2023 we have received a high volume of complaints about doctors' comments on social media related to the ongoing conflict in Gaza', but reiterated that 'Doctors are entitled to personal beliefs, and there is nothing preventing doctors from exercising their right to speak about or campaign on issues, but this must not affect their relationship with patients or the treatment they provide or arrange.'

The British Islamic Medical Association were concerned that doctors were being disciplined solely for airing pro-Palestine views. One NHS consultant, an advocate for Palestinian rights, has spoken about what he described as a persistent and orchestrated campaign of harassment. Despite multiple complaints being made against him, he was not found to have breached any professional standards.

The doctor raised the point that his social media posts condemning Russia's shelling of hospitals and support for Ukrainians had not attracted accusations of racism in the way his condemnation of attacks on hospitals in Gaza and support for the Palestinians had.

To some, Muslim casualties didn't matter.

The second recent moment that astonished me was the Nigel Farage 'debanking' furore.

Farage, the former leader of UKIP and current leader of Reform UK, has regularly made statements targeting Muslims. During the 2024 general election campaign, he said 'a growing number' of Muslims 'do not subscribe to British values' and 'loathe what we stand for'. He used a poll by the Henry Jackson Society as his justification to malign a whole community. He was challenged both on the lack of reliability of the HJS and the fact that survey research by IPSOS Mori, the largest and most credible on Muslim attitudes, showed that Muslims in the UK attach more importance to being British than do the general population.

This didn't stop Farage claiming that 'I could take you to streets in Oldham right now where no one speaks English' and that victorious Muslim candidates in the local elections earlier in the year shouted, 'We are coming to get you.'

Farage has history. He has said he would be uncomfortable living next door to a Romanian, compared Black Lives Matter protestors to the Taliban and called some British

Muslims a fifth column 'who hate us and want to kill us'. Despite Donald Trump's criminal conviction for thirty-four counts of falsifying business records to conceal 'hush money' to suppress information about sexual encounters, Farage remains a firm supporter of him. He is now an MP.

Coutts, a private bank owned by NatWest Group, closed Farage's account in 2023, claiming that he failed to meet the financial eligibility criteria and instead offered him a NatWest account.

It subsequently came to light that in an internal Coutts dossier Farage was described as a 'disingenuous grifter' who was 'xenophobic and pandering to racists'.

Though most are no fans of Farage, when the story broke some British Muslims were not altogether surprised by the bank's summary actions. Closure of bank accounts is a phenomenon that has blighted British Muslim organisations and individuals for a decade, with reports of high street banks such as HSBC closing accounts as far back as 2014.

Over the years I have had numerous contacts with individuals, organisations and banks on this issue. Both people and institutions have had services arbitrarily withdrawn and been left without any banking facilities, often not being able to function as a business or charity, or even manage day-to-day living.

Some have spoken publicly about this discrimination; others have not, fearing damage to their reputations and the impact it would have on their livelihoods. They did not have the privilege, platform or political support to mount the kind of campaign we saw on behalf of Farage.

According to Financial Conduct Authority data for 2022, the group most likely to be unbanked are Muslims; they are also most likely to be debanked.

Banks are not obliged to provide reasons for closure and there has been little recourse for those whose lives and livelihoods have been devastated by these actions. In February 2015, Peter Oborne resigned as the *Telegraph*'s chief political commentator. He had been reporting on HSBC closing British Muslims' bank accounts, a story which the paper failed to publish, despite, says Oborne, 'lawyers [being] unaware of any difficulty' in doing so. Oborne's piece, which was eventually published on the openDemocracy website in December 2014, details how Muslims as young as twelve had their accounts cancelled.

His investigations also found that World-Check, the database used by banks to justify their debanking decisions, flagged certain Muslim account holders as posing a 'terrorism' risk. World-Check, owned by Thomson Reuters, is used by forty-nine out of fifty of the world's biggest banks. Oborne found that it utilises sources of a dubious nature including state-sponsored news agencies in populating entries in its database. (World-Check insists the decisions to close accounts lies with the banks alone.)

Finsbury Park Mosque was one of the institutions that had an account cancelled and launched a successful legal challenge to get themselves removed from the World-Check database, securing an apology and damages from Thomson Reuters.

Some Muslim charities were given less than three months'

notice before their accounts were closed, with no explanation. The debanked charities were registered with the
Charity Commission, which did not have any concerns
about them.

Islamic Relief is one of the largest and longest-standing
Muslim charities in the country and is a member of the UK
Disasters Emergency Committee. In 2016, HSBC closed its
account, hindering the delivery of crucial aid in response to
the Nepal earthquake.

Another charity, Ummah Welfare Trust, was threatened
with bank closure during Ramadan, the month when
Muslims make the most donations to charity. At a meeting
with Antonio Simoes, HSBC's then UK chief executive, the
charity, which at the time turned over more than £20 million annually with HSBC, was told that 'pressure from the
UK and US governments' may have led to the bank's action.

In 2016, the Co-op Bank closed an account belonging
to Friends of Al-Aqsa, a British non-governmental organisation supporting Palestine. This, as reported in the
Independent, followed the closure of the accounts of 'as many
as twenty-five other Palestinian affiliated organisations including the Palestinian Solidarity Campaign'.

I accept banks are commercial organisations; they take
decisions based on risk. But what shocks me is the hypocrisy
and unequal treatment. When Nigel Farage had one of his
bank accounts closed and was offered another, the *Telegraph*
complained of a 'pernicious culture [that] has seeped
through the City and needs to be challenged now, not batted
away into a long-grass inquiry'. Yet when Muslims were

having all their bank accounts closed, the paper wanted to kill the story.

Senior media commentators including Andrew Neil and Piers Morgan piled in to defend Farage. Ministers raised the issue in Parliament. Prime Minister Rishi Sunak said it was 'not right' to deprive people of banking services because of their political views. The Chancellor of the Exchequer demanded an inquiry. The regulator, the Financial Conduct Authority, intervened. British banks were placed under the spotlight. Senior executives lost their jobs.

Yet when the Muslim debanking scandal broke, there were no ministerial statements about the injustice inflicted on our fellow British citizens, no calls for an inquiry into the banks' decisions, no support from high-profile politicians and commentators, no calls for resignations, no change of policy – because, unlike Nigel Farage, in the eyes of the powerful Muslims Don't Matter.

Let me move onto the third moment, which concerns that oft-cited British value: free speech.

The principle is regularly quoted at Muslims as a reason why Islam can be ridiculed, and why the most incendiary statements about Muslims are fair game. Yet free speech for Muslims has been curtailed by successive governments.

Allow me to unpick the rank hypocrisy and double standards where free speech is sometimes considered a fundamental right and sometimes a privilege.

In 2018, Toby Young was appointed to the Office for Students, the independent regulator for higher education in England. Young is an associate editor at the *Spectator*, a friend of Michael Gove's and was funded by the taxpayer to establish a free school in west London. Young's appointment, later described by the *Guardian* as 'flawed and rife with political interference', caused a backlash because of his history of homophobic, misogynistic and other offensive comments.

Young, who made many of these comments on Twitter, was alleged to have deleted forty thousand tweets, including offensive posts such as 'Fuck you, Penis breath' and 'smoking hot women . . . there should be an award for Best Baps' in relation to women attending the Emmys, and offensive comments about the cleavage of a female parliamentarian at Prime Minister's Questions. In the past, Young had also said working-class boys studying at the University of Oxford were 'universally unattractive' and 'small, vaguely deformed'.

(Interestingly his statements on Islam, including 'few people can be in any doubt that Islam is a deeply misogynistic religion', were not the basis of the outrage against him, because in the hierarchy of liberal outrage, Muslims don't feature.)

Senior political figures stepped forward to defend Young. His former editor at the *Spectator*, Boris Johnson, tweeted: 'Ridiculous outcry over Toby Young. He will bring independence, rigour and caustic wit. Ideal man for job'. Michael Gove agreed, tweeting 'how many of Toby Young's critics have worked night and day to provide great state schools for children of every background'. Unlike the Trojan Horse affair, where Gove led the charge against the unsavoury views of governors who presided over schools rated outstanding by Ofsted, it seems in this case he was prepared to overlook Young's unsavoury views.

Jo Johnson, younger brother of Boris Johnson and Universities Minister at the time, was reported to have personally encouraged Young to apply. When Young's tweets came to light, he dismissed suggestions that government departments should have waded through tweets 'made years – in some cases, decades – ago'.

Yet the government has for years maintained an Extremism Analysis Unit (now called Home Office Security Analysis and Insights) which does exactly this before any Muslim is allowed to engage with government, let alone be appointed in a formal role.

Young gave a robust defence of his past conduct: 'Given that defending free speech will be one of the Office for Students' priorities, there's a certain irony in people saying I'm "unfit" to serve on its board because of politically incorrect things I've said in the past. Some of those things have been sophomoric and silly – and I regret those – but some have been deliberately misinterpreted to try and paint me as a caricature of a heartless Tory toff.'

Such a defence is not a privilege afforded to British Muslims: they are not permitted to reject their past conduct as 'silly'. In fact, many British Muslims have been deliberately misinterpreted and caricatured as 'extremists' for their youthful posts by the very publications Young writes for.

I watch with amazement the indignation at 'cancel

culture' when applied to well-connected white male right-wing writers as contrasted to the enthusiastic application of it to Muslims. There is one rule for others and another higher standard for Muslims.

After pressure from the Labour Party and others, Toby Young stepped down, but he continued to enjoy the support of some of the most senior people in government and the media. When the appointment was investigated by the Commissioner for Public Appointments, he found evidence that 'demonstrated a lack of consistency in the approach to due diligence throughout this competition – it did not delve back extensively into his [Young's] social media, yet the social media activity of the initially preferred candidate for the student experience role was extensively examined'.

In fact, the Commissioner's report says one of the candidates was rejected because 'Ministers concluded that it would undermine the intended policy goals of the new regulator to appoint student representatives who publicly opposed the Prevent duty'.

So, one candidate was denied appointment because of their opposition to Prevent, a policy that stifles free speech. But the defence of free speech justified Young's appointment, with his declared caveat that offensive comments he had made in the past was 'sophomoric and silly'.

In 2023, the government announced the appointment of a 'free speech champion' to keep an eye on university campuses. It also continued to enforce the Prevent duty, which, since the Shawcross review, magnified Muslim 'extremists' as its main target rather than all forms of extremism.

We are now in a place where we champion free speech – just not for Muslims. The right to debate, disagree and dissent is a privilege afforded to the likes of Toby Young, who went on to set up the Free Speech Union, designed to defend victims of 'cancel culture'. It's an organisation that eventually found among its members the Islamophobe Tommy Robinson.

From economic disengagement to university applications and degree grading, from healthcare, to professional bodies and from banking to business to free speech, Muslims are being treated in ways others are not, damaging a community not fully able to play its part and damaging our country from the loss that follows.

It's a dangerously dehumanising place for British Muslims to be and it's why we urgently need to change course.

7

A Call for a Ceasefire

In 1894, Alfred Dreyfus, a French army captain from a successful and wealthy Jewish family, was wrongfully convicted of treason. The trial took place behind closed doors with a dossier of questionable evidence. Upon his arrest and in the run-up to the trial, newspapers printed wild conspiracy theories laced with antisemitic tropes and stereotypes focusing on the 'disgraceful treason of the Jew Dreyfus'.

Many used the moment to question the French state's decision to allow Jews to serve in the military and some agitated to bring back the death penalty for political crimes.

Dreyfus was unanimously convicted, sentenced to life imprisonment, paraded through the streets to chants of 'Death to Jews' and banished to serve his sentence on Devil's Island off the coast of French Guiana. Mathieu Dreyfus,

Alfred's older brother, said the experience 'seemed to us that we were no longer human beings like others'.

The Dreyfus family mounted a campaign to prove Alfred's innocence, which after many more miscarriages of justice eventually resulted in him being pardoned and reinstated into the military at a higher rank. He went on to serve in the First World War as an artillery major.

The Dreyfus affair, as it became known, was a very public manifestation of the widespread antisemitism in French society and politics where Jews were othered and their loyalty to the nation questioned. It exposed how instruments of the state colluded, the media enabled, and the public blindly followed a deeply bigoted ideology. (Ironically, one of the most rabidly anti-Dreyfus nationalistic newspapers was called *La Libre Parole*, or 'Free Speech').

Justice only prevailed when those with power and privilege spoke out. Figures such as Émile Zola, the distinguished novelist who published the famous *J'Accuse . . . !*, a detailed assessment of the rot that enabled the injustice; or General Georges-Gabriel de Pellieux, who conducted an unbiased investigation into the case; or the politicians who argued that France was behaving in ways contrary to French values; the newspapers which called for a retrial; ordinary French citizens who were not prepared to be taken in by divisive nationalism.

When even Jews who served in the armed forces were seen as traitors it left many Jews in France, as well as across Europe, questioning whether they would ever be accepted in their nations.

While the situation of Jews in nineteenth-century France is not exactly the same as Muslims in twenty-first-century Britain, I do see disturbing similarities both across Europe and here at home.

As an anti-racism activist in my early twenties, I did not imagine I would still be fighting the good fight for equal worth and value in my fifties. I did not think that in the 2024 general election, British Muslims would be treated as political fodder. I did not anticipate a climate where so many British Muslims were so marginalised that neither of the two main political parties felt like a comfortable home for them. I did not expect British Muslims to feel like the only way to be heard and be counted was by voting in substantial numbers for independent candidates. I did not anticipate seeing four British Muslims sitting in Parliament as independent MPs. Marginalised communities voting for individuals who find themselves marginalised in a system unable to accommodate them beyond the voice of an outsider.

I suppose what I did find completely predictable was the political and media hysteria and language of extremism and fear regarding the four Muslim independents (polling less than 2 per cent of the vote) and the lack of concern about five reform MPs, a party that managed to garner 14 per cent of the national vote.

The fact that both the Labour Party when it lost the red wall seats in the Midlands and the north of England and the Conservative Party when it lost votes to the Brexit Party or Reform felt it rightly necessary to try to reconnect with these 'white working-class' voters but neither felt the need to reconnect and reach out to Muslims when it lost constituencies with large Muslim populations to independents.

It seems Muslim votes don't matter.

Disengaged, excluded and judged according to standards other communities are not; stigmatised by our politicians and policymakers; stereotyped in media portrayals, culture, art, literature and film – in almost every aspect of life Muslims are told, you do not matter. You do not belong. You are the other, the outsider, the unusual and unable to be accommodated within the mainstream.

We are at a dangerous crossroads. I warned of the path we were walking in *The Enemy Within* with my closing sentence: 'The canaries in the coalmine are British Muslims.'

The war in Gaza was an inflection point where we saw with burning clarity the politicisation and dismissal of Muslim concerns. For the conflict to follow so soon after the Russian invasion of Ukraine and yet for our political response to be so markedly different.

From refugees' programmes to military support, from condemnation of Russian brutality and sanctions as well as political solidarity with the victims, we tangled ourselves in diplomatic and legal webs trying to justify a diametrically different stance over Israel in circumstances with many similarities.

The truth is that Muslims don't matter unless they are villains.

In the UK there is an abundance of policy, government attention and public funding to deal with extreme Muslims, difficult Muslims, homophobic Muslims, misogynistic

Muslims, intolerant Muslims, violent Muslims, politically non-compliant Muslims and even religiously too conservative Muslims. But Muslims who are killed, persecuted, isolated, discriminated against, victimised, politically excluded, denied freedom of religion and belief – they don't matter.

Having said at the outset that I would not caveat, apologise or explain in this book, I have felt myself being drawn into doing precisely that: clinging to facts, statistics and academic works to justify myself.

While writing, I have had to regularly pause and ask why I was, for example, making the case in Chapter 6 for Muslim economic engagement by referencing the loss to everyone else. Why, when making the case for tackling Islamophobia, I have referenced work on antisemitism or homophobia to persuade so-called liberal thinkers of the validity of the concept of anti-Muslim racism. Why, having said that British Muslims deserve to be seen as of equal worth and value, I still focused on non-Muslim self-interest rather than the injustice of anti-Muslim prejudice. It's because at each point I realised that Muslims Don't Matter.

Our economic exclusion is only relevant when it leads to an economic loss for others; our Plan Bs are only of interest when they lead to a brain and asset drain, our failure to be integrated into the mainstream only becomes an issue when it disturbs others; our disadvantage only requires attention when it hinders the majority.

It is time to reset – and I believe we can.

It requires long-term commitment, patience and a belief

that what makes us a nation is deeper than flags and fanfare. It's tragic that Rishi Sunak, the first prime minister of colour, presided over one of the most Islamophobic and divisive periods of Conservative Party history. Even when it was staring him in the face, Sunak was not able to use the word Islamophobia. His affront at being called a 'fucking Paki' by a Reform campaigner during the 2024 election felt a bit rich coming from a PM whose government has horribly demonised Pakistanis as 'groomers' and despite numerous requests failed to engage with British Pakistanis.

We need to listen to Muslims who have inhabited the public space and understand the challenges they have faced. The former First Minister of Scotland, Humza Yousaf, wrote an impassioned piece in the *Guardian* recently warning of the dangerous place we are in right now: 'Instead of challenging and confronting inflammatory anti-Muslim rhetoric, politicians have inexplicably allowed it to fester,' he warned. 'They have allowed anti-Muslim hate preachers to spread their insidious ideology and let it rip throughout our communities.'

Prominent Muslim Labour politicians back him up. Sadiq Khan has said: 'It is vital that our political parties lead from the front [in challenging Islamophobia] and set the strongest possible example to society.' And the Scottish Labour leader Anas Sarwar said of anti-Muslim hate: 'There are people in Scotland who feel scared to leave their homes for fear of verbal or physical attack, are withdrawing from public services with devastating knock-on consequences on their health and education and feel they are outsiders in their own country. This should shame us all.'

Despite being a Conservative, I am relieved and grateful that the country overwhelmingly rejected what my party had become in the 2024 general election. Its relationship with British Muslims was one of a multitude of issues it got terribly wrong.

The new Labour government has an opportunity to reset. So here is my advice to the new prime minister Keir Starmer.

A divided country may occasionally help win elections, but it doesn't build a nation.

We need to find ways that build an inclusive nationalism with a recognition of the good and bad of our nation's history. Not to erase all remnants of the past, not even to erase the celebrated statutes of those whose past isn't necessarily all to be celebrated; they are still a part of our history and should remain with added context of their actions, both good and bad.

We need to stop setting up 'existential' threats to our country – judges, human rights, the wrong kind of refugees – and focus on how we are undermining the very values we are seeking to preserve: democracy, the rule of law and an international rule-based system.

We need political leaders who are not easily persuaded by populism and are not prepared to cast aside their values; politicians who don't see Muslims as collateral damage in winning an election, thoughtlessly thrown under the campaign bus. We need politicians who actively work to create understanding, to prevent suspicion and hatred, who encourage us to reach across our divides and do not entrench them for political gain.

In an election year where Muslims have been fair game,

I want the new government to cut through the toxic debate and remake the case for a multicultural, inclusive, tolerant country. In a year when mobs have taken to the streets attacking mosques and setting fire to libraries, and 'Paki-bashing' has returned to our streets, the government needs to send the clear message that British Muslims are an integral part of our nation.

We need to find ways to walk in other people's shoes, to create space for conversations like we do on *A Muslim and a Jew Go There*, to speak in ways which are both civil and civilising.

We need to stop holding British Muslims to standards we do not demand of others. Much like Jewish and Christian religious texts, Islamic scripture taken out of context can be painted as irredeemably alien. Two pranksters in Denmark demonstrated this in their 'Quran experiment', reading verses from the Bible as though they were from the Quran and asking their European audience to react. Most responded negatively – until the identity of the text was revealed.

Whether because of absurd cultural practices, criminality or plain stupidity, every community has individuals it would like to disown – I've spent most of my life challenging and fighting them in the Muslim community. But just as Jimmy Savile is not a reflection of all white men and Harvey Weinstein or Jeffrey Epstein are not a reflection of all Jewish men, so Abu Hamza should not be seen as a reflection of all Muslim men. It's time to challenge group accountability for British Muslims and stop comparing the worst of one community to the best of another.

Sometimes it seems the very things we celebrate in non-Muslim people are the ones we despise in Muslims. Qualities we yearn for like family values, community, inter-generational support, charity or the behaviours we so admired in the late Queen – modesty, reserve, faith, conservative social values – are exactly the ones we despise in Muslim women.

Both the government and the media need to reflect on their approach. We need to be prepared to challenge double standards as I did with the BBC.

Question Time is an important platform and yet it has chosen to invite individuals who have perpetuated stereotypes about Muslims – among them Jake Wallis Simons, Melanie Phillips, Douglas Murray and Nigel Farage. And yet it came under pressure from government and cancelled an appearance by Zara Mohammed, the secretary-general of the Muslim Council of Britain, because of the government's policy of disengagement with the organisation.

It's time for all fair-minded, right-thinking people to speak up. It's time to end culture wars that support a very particular interpretation of a society's political fault lines.

Culture wars aren't just an ugly political phenomenon. They are deeply dangerous and, as we are seeing in the US, have the potential to reverse our bumpy journey towards a liberal, inclusive society. And there is no doubt that, across the world, Muslims are the main target of these culture wars, seen as the ones to unite against, the focus of political rhetoric and ever more draconian and exclusionary laws.

Across the world populists are reducing complex political issues to simplistic questions of belonging, and then framing any disagreement as illegitimate. Often, they call themselves patriots and defenders of the 'ordinary man' against a 'liberal elite', who they define as out of touch at best and traitors at worst.

Those dismissed as being in the 'elite' camp are often anything but elite – for example, in the US Black men who are victims of police brutality – while those representing the 'ordinary man', Trump or Modi for example, are the top of society. Such leaders use culture wars to place on the back burner the need to find economic answers to economic challenges – challenges faced both by the victimised group, such as British Muslims, and those mobilised against them, such as poor white communities. Economic polarisation plays out through symbolic polarisation.

Both sides of the present divide feel unheard, marginalised and are outraged – an outrage fed by the media and politicians for clicks, views and votes. The result is that the economically disadvantaged blame their fellow citizens for the situation rather than those in power.

Populists divide citizens into homogeneous groups, seeking to define the authentic citizen – the patriot, in contrast to groups that don't belong. And all the while making political gain off the back of division. Worldwide, this approach often triggers disharmony, sometimes violence, and in extreme cases genocide: the Rohingya community in Burma is a stark example.

We are a liberal democracy with a long and proud history, and we demean ourselves by adopting an authoritarian approach to a section of our fellow citizens. We undermine our stated values, and we appear as hypocrites. This must stop.

We still have an opportunity to reset and protect all who make up our country.

I have argued for many years that national cohesion is as necessary as national security and needs to be funded and supported as such. For over a decade I have argued for a specific department that unites our four nations and the diverse communities within them, a Department for National Identity and Integration. Keir Starmer in the 2024 election campaign spoke of his desire to bring the country together. I agree. But these words need to translate into action, supported by political will and be properly resourced.

The Culture Secretary, Lisa Nandy, said within hours of her appointment 'the era of culture wars is over'. I welcome this. We must also alongside this celebrate an inclusive, vibrant, tolerant multicultural Britain.

Muslims need to be welcomed back into the mainstream of policymaking and that starts with tackling anti-Muslim racism both in communities and within government.

The new Labour government should formally adopt the definition of Islamophobia, work that was led by Wes Streeting and something Labour committed to in opposition. Islamophobia, let us not forget, is a form of racism that targets expressions of Muslimness or perceived Muslimness, a definition which is neither religious nor theologically based, and like the definition of antisemitism adopted by both parties expressly seeks to protect people, not a particular faith. Both are non-legally binding working definitions that signal intent and a direction of travel. Both encourage acceptance through cultural change rather than criminalisation.

In addition, we need a determined and concerted effort to address Islamophobia across all sectors of politics, economy, education, healthcare and society. The Labour government should make good on its promise to tackle employment discrimination and wage disparity and introduce manda-tory reporting on the Ethnicity Pay Gap as we have done for gender.

The government should establish an independent in-quiry into the Trojan Horse affair, to bring full closure to the whole disgraceful episode and to identify the areas and actors that failed our children in Birmingham and to learn lessons for the future.

It's also time to return Prevent to its original limited aim and subject it to external scrutiny and oversight. It's time to repeal the Prevent statutory duty and mainstream this work into safeguarding where it belongs. Equally applied, evidentially led and with a focus on preventing criminality not policing thoughts and opinions this must be a policy that both keeps us safe and protects our freedoms.

Labour should re-establish the principle that all British citizens have the same class of citizenship and bring

Shamima Begum back to Britain to face justice in her home country. All the other women and children who continue to languish in Syria must also be returned. The rest of the world have taken back theirs and we need to take back ours.

The new Labour government must respond anew to the Sir Duncan Ouseley review on closed material proceedings and adopt the recommendations, including those of the special advocates. It must establish robust oversight on legal processes and procedures that if we must deviate from the rules of natural justice, it is only in exceptional circumstances and in a limited way.

The government should implement a workable process for press regulation. Over a decade on from the Leveson Inquiry, the recommendations remain ignored.

We must end the government policy of disengagement and allow British Muslims the agency of their own representatives as we do for every other community.

We must decouple easy, lazy, populist answers from a pragmatic, workable solution rooted in our values. We must push back against attempts to silence, subjugate and stereotype our fellow citizens.

It's time to return to evidence-based policymaking, not shaped by the dangerous axis of influence made up of think tanks and lobby groups with an agenda of marginalising Muslims.

And all of us must challenge media narratives that defame and libel. To question the story rather than judge a whole community. When discussing all things Muslim, we should use Tariq Modood's checklist as laid out in Chapter 1, and my test – swap the community in question and see how it feels and sounds. Demand that consequences flow for the prolific offenders in politics, media and public life who malign Muslims and feed division.

And to my fellow Muslims, be brave enough to say, *I'm done*. Say to newspapers, broadcasters and individuals, especially those with a history of Islamophobia, that you have no right to hold me accountable and no right to judge me to a higher standard than the one you apply to yourselves. Do not apologise, caveat, explain or defend – we are not collectively responsible. Do not be backed into a corner by the disingenuous, the prolific offender, the Islamophobe. Tell our fellow Brits exactly how you feel. Tell your story on your terms, in your way, at a time that suits you.

I have great faith in my country and its people. Once the poisoned tap of culture wars is turned off, once those in leadership stop feeding hate, ordinary people will embrace British Muslims as many have embraced them now. Whether it's our *Bake Off* queen Nadiya Hussain, World Cup-winning cricketer Moeen Ali, the Egyptian king in Liverpool Mo Salah, multiple gold medal-winning Olympian Sir Mo Farah, Saliha Mahmood-Ahmed the gastro doctor and *MasterChef* winner, the new David Attenborough and rhythm personified Hamza Yassin, winner of *Strictly Come Dancing*, or Asmaa Al-Allak, the surgeon and seamstress extraordinaire who won *The Great British Sewing Bee*, many Muslims are our national heroes. As my friend the former Conservative MP for High Wycombe

Steve Baker said, 'They deserve better than to be the object of this clear and intolerable bigotry.'

Throughout this book I have sought to reflect the private conversations of so many British Muslims. The fear in communities is deep: Plan B exit routes are being prepared. The paralysis and feeling of being silenced is stifling. And these anxious, fearful, hushed conversations have gone on for too long.

I want you, the reader, to be as outraged as I am. I want you to demand that Islamophobia is taken as seriously as antisemitism, anti-black racism and homophobia – to be socially unacceptable and have the same legal framework as other forms of racism.

I have thought long and hard about what I have said, and I am asking well-intentioned, thoughtful and liberal people to think again.

Nearly seventy years after my family's in-country rela-tionship with Britain started, and four generations later, I refuse to accept that my country may not be home to my grandchildren and their children. My grandfathers did not give their blood and sweat for their descendants to be stereotyped, stigmatised and silenced. They did not make sacrifices for the freedoms we enjoy today to see their future generations deprived of those very liberties. They did not give their loyalty to this nation for the baying mob in 2024 to accuse their offspring of disloyalty and demand a purge.

They fought for Britain, helped build Britain's industries and infrastructure, added colour, sounds and wonderful flavours to the rich tapestry of its culture. As a young and growing community, British Muslims are once again providing the workforce, entrepreneurs and thinkers to, if I may repurpose a phrase for better use, make Britain great again.

It's time for Muslims to Matter.

Notes

1: Buying Diamonds

2   *'bank robbers':* Boris Johnson, 'Denmark has got it wrong.
        Yes, the burka is oppressive and ridiculous – but that's
        still no reason to ban it', *Telegraph*, 5 August 2018.

3   *Suella Braverman write for* The Times*:* Suella Braverman,
        'Police must be even-handed with protests', *The Times*,
        8 November 2023.

3   *Lee Anderson, claimed:* GB News, 23 February 2024.

3   *Robert Peston pointed out: Peston*, ITV, 20 March 2024.

5   *'made a detailed plan':* 'Right-wing supremacist
        sentenced over plot to kill worshipping Muslims
        while disguised as armed police officer', CPS, 10
        November 2023.

5   *'idolised':* Chloe Laversuch, 'Joe Metcalfe jailed for
        plotting mosque terror attack dressed as PC', BBC
        News, 10 November 2023.

8   *'Islamophobia is rooted in racism':* 'Islamophobia
        Defined: The Inquiry into a Working Definition
        of Islamophobia/Anti-Muslim Hatred', All-Party
        Parliamentary Group on British Muslims, 2018.

10   *'did it for Lee Rigby'*: Steven Morris and agency, 'Nazi-obsessed loner guilty of attempted murder of dentist in racist attack', *Guardian*, 25 June 2015.

10   *'pretty good' joke*: Rowan Atkinson, letter to *The Times*, 10 August 2018.

11   *Professor Tariq Modood . . . series of tests*: Tariq Modood, 'What Is Islamophobia?', written evidence (HCL0057) to Islamophobia inquiry, Parliament.uk.

12   *'Christian child forced'*: Andrew Norfolk, 'Christian child forced into Muslim foster care', *The Times*, 28 August 2017.

12   *'vigilante action'*: 'Tommy Robinson encouraged "vigilante action" in Facebook Live', BBC News, 9 July 2019.

12–13   *'don't think that their [white male] actions'*: Reni Eddo-Lodge, *Why I'm No Longer Talking to White People About Race* (London: Bloomsbury, 2017).

14   *'based on the existing evidence'*: 'Group-based Child Sexual Exploitation Characteristics of Offending', Home Office, December 2020.

15   *'family heritage is Muslim'*: Andrew Grice, 'Sajid Javid – profile: the working class Conservative taking over from Maria Miller as Culture Secretary', *Independent*, 9 April 2014.

16   *'almost all British Pakistani men'*: Glen Owen, 'Suella Braverman vows to stamp out grooming gangs behind organised child sex abuse', *Mail on Sunday*, 1 April/24 September 2023.

17   *'obsessed'*: Quoted in 'Finsbury Park: Man "wanted to kill Muslims in van attack"', BBC News, 22 January 2018.

18   *'My own view'*: Rod Liddle, 'Why Boris is wrong about Burkas', *Spectator*, 11 August 2018.

18   *'I'm an Islamophobe':* Polly Toynbee, 'I'm an Islamophobe – and proud of it', *Independent*, 23 October 1997.

18   *'only the objection':* Christopher Hitchens, 'Freedom of Speech – Resisting Islam', YouTube, 2012.

19   *'Islamophobia is a word':* Andrew Cummins, quoted in Matt Cerami, 'Fascists, cowards, and morons: Combating anti-Muslim bigotry while maintaining free speech', *The Humanist*, 28 July 2015.

19   *'Islamophobia builds imaginary constructs':* Quoted in 'UN expert says anti-Muslim hatred rises to epidemic proportions, urges States to act', press release, UN Human Rights Office of the High Commissioner, 4 March 2021.

20   *Trevor Phillips claimed in 2016:* Trevor Phillips, with commentaries from David Goodhart and Jon Gower Davies, *Race and Faith: The Deafening Silence* (London: Civitas, 2016).

20   *'see the world differently':* Quoted in 'UK Muslims see world differently from the rest of us, says former equalities chief', Middle East Eye, 27 January 2016.

20   *'becoming a nation within a nation':* Quoted in David Barrett, 'British Muslims becoming a nation within a nation, Trevor Phillips warns', *Telegraph*, 11 April 2016.

20   *'I thought Europe's Muslims':* Quoted in 'One in four Muslims "backing Sharia law"', *Herald*, 11 April 2016.

21   *'[If] you do belong to a group':* Haroon Siddique, 'Labour lifts Trevor Phillips' suspension for alleged Islamophobia', *Guardian*, 6 July 2021.

21   *'This is plain and simple':* Richard Ferrer, 'Regime-change invasion is surely only hours away and with it the end of Hamas', *Daily Express*, 10 October 2023.

22   *'I try not to use phrases':* 'Table Talk with David
        Cameron', *emel Magazine*, 30 (March 2007).

2: The Rotten State

30   *'non-evidence based':* Claystone Associates, written
        evidence (PCB0004) to Draft Protection of
        Charities Bill Joint Committee, Parliament.uk, 11
        December 2014.
30   *'We simply do not wish':* William Shawcross, 'Yes,
        the problem is "Islamic fascism"', *Jerusalem Post*, 13
        August 2006.
31   *'conditions for Muslims':* Douglas Murray, speech, Pym
        Fortuyn Memorial Conference on Europe and Islam,
        The Hague, February 2006.
32   *'repeatedly apologised':* 'Shaima Dallali – National Union
        of Students', press release, Carter-Ruck Solicitors, 7
        May 2024.
33   *'I trust that you will consult':* Marie van der Zyl, by
        e-mail to the Rt Hon Michael Gove, MP, 14 March
        2024. Reproduced at 'Board President's letter of
        support for Lord Mann, Independent Adviser on
        Antisemitism', Board of Deputies of British Jews, 14
        March 2024.
34   *'dodgy judgement':* Claire Ellicott, 'Penny Mordaunt
        flouted No. 10 ban to meet boycotted group:
        Tory leadership hopeful is condemned for "dodgy
        judgment" ahead of MPs' vote tonight – after rivals
        clash in feisty TV debate', *Daily Mail*, 17 July 2022.
34   *'Cometh the hour':* Jason Groves, 'Cometh the hour,
        cometh the woman . . .', *Daily Mail*, 6 September 2022.
35   *'fundamental British values':* Prevent Strategy, HM
        Government, June 2011.

36   *'the enemy at the table':* Douglas Murray, 'After Woolwich, what will change?', *Spectator*, 1 June 2013.

36   *'Islamic "radicals"':* Andrew Gilligan, 'Islamic "radicals" at the heart of Whitehall, *Telegraph*, 22 February 2015.

38   *'wrong', 'unacceptable, 'ill judged':* Quoted in Zoe Grunewald, 'Sunak says Lee Anderson comments were wrong but denies Conservative party has "Islamophobic tendencies"', *Independent*, 26 February 2024.

38   *'I try . . .':* Graeme Demianyk, 'Iain Dale delivers withering takedown of "serial offender" Lee Anderson', *HuffPost*, 27 February 2024.

38–9   *'I used to think':* Politics Live, BBC, 28 February 2024.

39   *'completely unfounded allegations':* 'Jewish Chronicle, Stephen Pollard and Lee Harpin apologise and pay substantial libel damages to Nada al-Sanjari', press release, Carter-Ruck Solicitors, 6 October 2020.

40   *'an enthusiastic combatant':* Daniel Thomas and Harriet Agnew, 'Paul Marshall's evolution from financier to media baron', *Financial Times*, 8 March 2024.

41   *'one-note theme':* Gavin Esler, 'GB spews', *Prospect*, May 2024 (online 27 March 2024).

41   *do not 'represent his views':* Quoted in Gregory Davis, 'Revealed: The shocking tweets of GB News co-owner Sir Paul Marshall', Hope Not Hate, 22 February 2024.

42   *'bank robbers' or 'letter boxes':* Johnson, 'Denmark has got it wrong'.

42   *'The article did not include':* '05935-16 Manji v The Sun', IPSO ruling, 19 October 2016.

43   *'Islam threatens the British way of life':* Stephen H. Jones and Amy Unsworth, 'The Dinner Table Prejudice: Islamophobia in Contemporary Britain', University of Birmingham, 2022.

44   *'There is a fundamental clash':* GB Tracker: Islam and
        British value, YouGov.
44   *'Muslims are taking over England':* See Matthew Taylor,
        'Racist and anti-immigration views held by children
        revealed in schools study', *Guardian*, 19 May 2015.
44   *'horrified':* Richard Dawkins, 'I'm a Cultural Christian',
        LBC via YouTube, 1 April 2024.
45   *'creeping erosion':* TalkTV via YouTube, 28 March 2024.
45   *'traditional submissiveness':* Laura Hughes, 'David
        Cameron: More Muslim women should "learn
        English" to help tackle extremism', *Telegraph*, 17
        January 2016.
46   *'seek to de-escalate', 'Perhaps the honourable lady':* Hansard,
        15 January 2024.
46   *'Feminist activists would be foolish':* Eddo-Lodge, *Why I'm
        No Longer Talking to White People About Race.*

3: The Dinner Table Test

50   *'We must not stoop':* David Cameron, JP Morgan
        lecture, British American Project, 11 September 2006.
        Transcript at 'In full: Cameron on foreign policy', BBC
        News, 11 September 2006.
50   *'uneasy talking to someone':* Jack Straw, 'I felt uneasy
        talking to someone I couldn't see', *Guardian*, 6
        October 2006.
53   *'I have never used those words':* @Mark_Spencer, Twitter,
        22 January 2022.
57   *'Indian Kashmir has now':* Swaran Singh, 'Kashmir: a
        tale of two mothers', *Spiked*, 13 August 2019.
57   *'"Islamophobia" is an elite invention':* Brendon O'Neill,
        'No, Islamophobia is not the new anti-Semitism',
        Spiked, 6 June 2018.

58   *'we need to junk':* Wasiq Wasiq, 'We need to junk the
        idea of "Islamophobia"', *Spiked*, 14 July 2020.

60   *'hierarchy of racism':* The Forde Report, Labour Party, 19
        July 2022.

60   *'anti-black racism and Islamophobia':* Aletha Adu, 'Labour
        accused of still not engaging with "hierarchy of
        racism" claims', *Guardian*, 18 March 2023.

60   *'how a British political party':* Al Jazeera Investigative
        Unit, 'Documents reveal discrimination and racism in
        UK Labour Party', *Al Jazeera*, 29 September 2022.

60   *'We're haemorrhaging votes':* Dan Hodges, 'Who's
        spreading the poison that could put the final nail
        in Keir Starmer's coffin?', *Mail on Sunday*, 19/20
        June 2021.

60   *'a patently vile Islamophobic briefing':* @LabourMuslims,
        Twitter, 20 June 2021.

60   *'shaking off the fleas':* Quoted in Kiran Stacey, Aletha Adu
        and Ben Quinn, 'Labour deeply divided over Starmer's
        line on Israel–Hamas war', *Guardian*, 20 October 2023.

4: Unpopular Culture

66   *'displaying Blackness':* John Strausbaugh, *Black Like
        You: Blackface, Whiteface, Insult & Imitation in American
        Popular Culture* (New York: Tarcher, 2006).

67   *'Arabs are the most maligned':* Jack G. Shaheen, *Reel Bad
        Arabs: How Hollywood Vilifies a People* (New York:
        Olive Branch Press, 2012, revised edn).

68   *'because [these films] focus':* Marloes Veldhausz,
        'Constructing Islamophobia: Hollywood', master's
        thesis, Radboud University, 2017.

69   *'in an effort', Comments on social networks:* Quoted in
        Nicky Wolf, 'American Sniper: Anti-Muslim threats

skyrocket in wake of film's release', *Guardian*, 24 January 2015.

69   *'scandalously blinkered':* David Edelstein, 'Clint Eastwood turns *American Sniper* into a Republican platform movie', *New York*, 16 January 2015.

69   *'the biggest antiwar statement':* Quoted in Gregg Kilday, 'Clint Eastwood on *American Sniper*'s "biggest antiwar statement', *Hollywood Reporter*, 24 January 2015.

69   *'it seems that the only good Iraqi':* Jordan Elgrably, '"American Sniper" not only inflames anti-Muslim behavior, but is a botched film', blog post, jordanelgrably.com, 4 February 2015.

70   *'a new kind of unabashedly bigoted blockbuster':* Kaashif Hajee, 'Saffronizing Bollywood: How India's Hindu right is controlling its prolific film industry', blog post, SOAS, 3 May 2024.

70   *'thinly veiled propaganda':* Mukund Setlur, '"Article 370" movie review: Another thinly veiled propaganda film', *Deccan Herald*, 23 February 2024.

71   *'infiltrators', 'termites':* Quoted in Hugh Tomlinson, 'Narendra Modi gives BJP chief Amit Shah, who called Muslims "termites", top cabinet job', *The Times*, 1 June 2019.

71   *'Monochromatic depictions':* Sam Gill, 'The "brute math" behind Hollywood's outsized role in shaping perceptions of Muslims and Jews in America', *Hollywood Reporter*, 9 February 2024.

74   *'I have not been able to discover':* Edward W. Said, 'Islam through Western eyes', *The Nation*, 26 April 1980.

74   *'What can we do':* Martin Amis, interviewed by Ginny Dougary, *The Times*, September 2006. Quoted in Maev Kennedy, 'Enough, says Amis, in Eagleton feud', *Guardian*, 13 October 2007.

75   *'[T]he impulse towards rational inquiry'*: Martin Amis,
      'The age of horrorism', *Observer*, 10 September 2006.
75   *'pseudo-scholarship and fanatical conviction'*: Pankaj
      Mishra, 'The politics of paranoia', *Observer*, 17
      September 2006.
75   *'nurtures in his audience'*: Chris Morris, 'The absurd
      world of Martin Amis', *Observer*, 25 November 2007.
76   *'sounded like a threat'*: Howard Jacobson, 'When you've
      got a red-top heart, the concept of human rights means
      absolutely nothing', *Independent*, 13 August 2005.
76–7 *'the same image'*: *Newsnight* via YouTube, 17
      February 2024.
77   *Lionel Shriver . . . went on* Question Time: Aaya
      Al-Shamahi and Khaled Shalaby, 'Lionel Shriver
      grilled on *Question Time*', Middle East Eye, 29
      November 2019.
77   *'the native-born'*: Lionel Shriver, 'Would you want
      London to be overrun with Americans like me?',
      Spectator, 28 August 2021.
78   *'stupidest religion'*: 'Houellebecq acquitted of insulting
      Islam', *Guardian*, 22 October 2002.
80   *'on London stages in every decade'*: Matthew Dimmock,
      'The troubled history of putting Islam on stage',
      Prospect, 12 June 2015.
80   *'The Indian Mussulmans'*: Raffiuddin Ahman, letter
      to *The Times*, 26 September 1883. Quoted in Kristan
      Tetens, 'The Lyceum and the Lord Chamberlain: The
      case of Hall Caine's *Mahomet*', in Richard Foulkes
      (ed.), *Henry Irving: A Re-Evaluation of the Pre-Eminent
      Victorian Actor-Manager* (Abingdon: Routledge, 2018).
80–1 *'pray assure all of whom'*: Quoted in ibid.
82   *'The bizarre act'*: 'The bizarre act that ruined the
      greatest moment in World Cup history', changed to

'Lionel Messi made to wear traditional Arab robe for World Cup trophy lift', *Telegraph*, 18 December 2022.

83   *'We're having a lovely time':* Angela Rafferty and Dan Martin, 'Derby football fans in Qatar set for World Cup clash with France', BBC News, 10 December 2022.

84   *gave a horrifying account:* Azim Rafiq, witness statement to DCMS Committee, Parliament.uk, 16 November 2021. Reported in Sean Ingle, 'Azeem Rafiq tells MPs that "inhuman" racist abuse cost him cricket career', *Guardian*, 16 November 2021.

85   *'Headingley is less welcoming':* Quoted in 'England & Wales Cricket Board Limited and Yorkshire County Cricket Club: Decision of the Disciplinary Panel as to Sanction', England and Wales Cricket Board.

85   *'banter':* 'Statement from Chair of Yorkshire Country Cricket Club Roger Hutton on Behalf of the Club Together with a Summary of the Panel's Report and Recommendations', Yorkshire CCC, 10 September 2021.

85   *'inappropriate behaviour':* 'Club Statement', Yorkshire CCC, 19 August 2021.

85   *Cricket Scotland . . . 'institutionally racist':* 'Changing the boundaries report into racism in Scottish Cricket April update', SportScotland, 28 April 2022.

86   *'the luck of an Irishman':* Max McLean, 'Eoin Morgan says "We had Allah with us" as captain praises England's diversity', Yahoo! News, 15 July 2019.

87   *'these results may be driven':* 'Salah helping to reduce hate crime, says study', Premier League, 5 June 2019.

87   *the 'Riz Test':* 'What is the Riz Test?' at riztest.com.

5: Blind Injustice

94   *'registration as an entitlement':* Hansard, 2 June 1981.

96   *'a person accused of speeding':* Quoted in Haroon Siddique, 'New bill quietly gives powers to remove British citizenship without notice', *Guardian*, 17 November 2021.

97   *'a fundamentally racist policy':* Jacob Rees-Mogg, 'Shamima Begum shouldn't have lost her British citizenship', *Spectator*, 24 February 2024.

98   *'although we may':* Bonnie Honig, 'A Legacy of Xenophobia', *Boston Review*, 1 December 2002.

99   *'Those with no right':* Rees-Mogg, 'Shamima Begum shouldn't have lost her British citizenship'.

100   *identified as 'at risk':* Duncan Gardham, 'Shamima Begum: Police and school "missed opportunities" to stop her leaving UK, lawyers claim', Sky News, 22 November 2022.

101   *'no question':* 'Shamima Begum will not be allowed here, Bangladesh says', BBC News, 21 February 2019.

101   *'Not only does Britain':* Bobbie Mills, 'Citizenship deprivation: How Britain took the lead on dismantling citizenship', European Network on Statelessness, 3 March 2016.

102   *'He will be subject':* Philip Hensher, 'It's wrong to strip Abu Hamza of his citizenship', *Independent*, 3 April 2003.

106   *'co-ordinated, deliberate and sustained action':* Peter Clarke, 'Report into allegations concerning Birmingham schools arising from the "Trojan Horse" letter', House of Commons, July 2014.

107   *'set up', 'cooker bomb':* 'Eroding Trust: The UK's Prevent Counter-Extremism Strategy in Health and Education', Open Society Justice Initiative, 2016.

107   *'If he was dressed in black'*: Quoted in ibid.

108   *'confused epic of simplistic incomprehension'*: William
        Dalrymple, review, *Sunday Times*, September 2006.

109   *'a sizeable minority'*: Michael Gove, *Celsius 7/7* (London:
        Weidenfeld & Nicolson, 2006).

109   *'desperately unfortunate'*, *'divert attention'*: 'Trojan Horse
        probe headed by ex-Met chief Peter Clarke', BBC
        News, 15 April 2014.

110   *'a number of people'*: Clarke, 'Report into allegations
        concerning Birmingham schools arising from the
        "Trojan Horse" letter'.

110   *'no evidence of a conspiracy'*: Quoted in Helen Pidd and
        Richard Adams, 'Birmingham council a "disastrous
        failure" over Islamism in schools', *Guardian*, 18 July
        2014.

110   *'plot'*: Quoted in 'Trojan Horse: 25 schools probed over
        alleged takeover plot', BBC News, 14 April 2014.

110   *'all schools should be like this'*, *'witch hunt'*: 'Extremism
        in schools: the Trojan Horse affair', Education
        Committee, Parliament.uk.

111   *'it offended her as a Muslim'*: Frances Perraudin, 'Muslim
        teaching assistant wins unfair dismissal case over 9/11
        footage', *Guardian*, 31 October 2017.

113   *'Injustice anywhere'*: Martin Luther King Jr, 'Letter from
        a Birmingham Jail', 16 April 1963.

6: Unequal Nation

116   *'religious freedom contributes'*: Brian J. Grim, Greg Clark
        and Robert Edward Snyder, 'Is Religious Freedom
        Good for Business? A Conceptual and Empirical
        Analysis', *Interdisciplinary Journal of Research on Religion*,
        10 (2014).

116   *'innovative strength'*: Brian J. Grim, 'The link between economic and religious freedoms', World Economic Forum, 18 December 2014.

119   *'The report underlines'*: Quoted in 'Government must tackle inequalities faced by Muslim people in employment', Parliament.uk, 11 August 2016.

119   *'stereotypical views', 'triple penalty'*: 'Employment Opportunities for Muslims in the UK', Women and Equalities Committee, Second Report of Session 2016–17, Parliament.uk.

119–20 *'the government needs'*: 'Government must tackle inequalities faced by Muslim people in employment', Women and Equalities Committee, Parliament.uk, 11 August 2016.

120   *'pay particular attention'*: 'Employment Opportunities for Muslims in the UK'.

121   *'more needs to be done'*: Citizens Commission on Islam, Participation and Public Life, 'The Missing Muslims: Unlocking British Muslim Potential for the Benefit of All', Citizens UK, 2017.

121–2   *'racism and discrimination'*: Jacqueline Stevenson et al., 'The Social Mobility Challenges Faced by Young Muslims', Social Mobility Commission, September 20170

122   *'if you are a Muslim'*: Nabil Khattab and Tariq Modood, 'Both Ethnic and Religious: Explaining Employment Penalties Across 14 Ethno-Religious Groups in the United Kingdom', *Journal for the Scientific Study of Religion*, 54:3 (2015).

124   *'highest age-standardised mortality rates'*: Muslim Council of Britain, written submission (CVB0006), Parliament.uk.

124   *'vast majority', 'mosques and imams', 'beach lovers'*: Quoted

in 'Craig Whittaker: MP defends saying some Muslims not taking covid seriously', BBC News, 31 July 2020.

127   *'[s]ince October 2023'*: Quoted in Gabriella Swerling, 'Dozens of doctors accused of anti-Semitism', *Telegraph* via Yahoo! News, 9 May 2024.

128   *'a growing number'*: Quoted in Alix Cuthbertson, 'Nigel Farage called out for "blanket accusation" as he says "growing number" of Muslims "loathe" British values', Sky News, 27 May 2024.

128   *'I could take you'*: Quoted in James Gregory and Sophie Abdulla (eds), 'Keir Starmer says Rishi Sunak had "back against the wall" and lied in debate', BBC News, 4 June 202.

128   *'We are coming to get you'*: Quoted in Peter Walker, 'Reality check: how do Farage's claims on immigration, economy and crime hold up?', *Guardian*, 3 June 2024.

129   *'who hate us and want to kill us'*: Quoted in Matt Dathan, 'Nigel Farage: "Some Muslims want to kill us"', *Independent*, 12 March 2015.

129   *'disingenuous grifter'*, *'xenophobic'*: 'Key points from Coutts' dossier on Nigel Farage', Sky News, 28 July 2023.

130   *'lawyers [being] unaware'*: Peter Oborne, 'Why I have resigned from the *Telegraph*', openDemocracy, 17 February 2015.

131   *'pressure from the UK'*: Quoted in Peter Oborne and Alex Delmar-Morgan, 'Open for business?', openDemocracy, 19 December 2014.

131   *'as many as twenty-five'*: Hazel Sheffield, 'Co-op Bank shuts down account belonging to Palestinian NGO Friends of Al-Aqsa "without explanation"', *Independent*, 6 January 2016.

131   *'pernicious culture [that] has seeped'*: 'Banking's problem is bigger than NatWest', *Telegraph*, 26 July 2023.

132   *'not right'*: '"Not right" to deprive people of bank accounts because of their views – Sunak', Sky News via YouTube, 27 July 2023.

133   *'flawed and rife with political interference'*: Richard Adams, 'Ministers meddled in Toby Young getting OfS role, report finds', *Guardian*, 26 February 2018.

133   *'universally unattractive'*: Toby Young, in Rachel Johnson (ed.), *The Oxford Myth* (London: Weidenfeld & Nicolson, 1988).

133   *'few people can be in any doubt'*: Toby Young, 'By refusing to ban the burka, Damian Green is supporting the humiliation of millions of British women', *Telegraph*, July 2010.

134   *'made years – in some cases, decades – ago'*: Hansard, 8 January 2018.

134   *'Given that defending free speech'*: Quoted in Ashley Cowburn, 'Toby Young deletes thousands of tweets amid row over his universities regulator appointment', *Independent*, 3 January 2018.

135   *'demonstrated a lack of consistency'*: 'The Commissioner for Public Appointments Report on the Recruitment Campaign for the Office for Students', The Commissioner for Public Appointments, February 2018.

7: A Call for a Ceasefire

137   *'disgraceful treason of the Jew Dreyfus'*: Edouard Drumont, *La Libre Parole*, 3 November 1894.

138   *'seemed to us'*: Mathieu Dreyfus, *The Affair That I Have Lived* (Paris: Bernard Grasset, 1978).

142   *'Instead of challenging'*: Humza Yousaf, 'I was the first

Muslim leader of a western democracy. And I say Islamophobia has poisoned our politics', *Guardian*, 17 June 2024.

142   *'It is vital':* Quoted in Michael Savage, 'Sadiq Khan challenges Theresa May to act against Tory Islamophobia', *Observer*, 24 March 2019.

142   *'There are people in Scotland':* Quoted in 'Anas Sawar: "Islamophobia in Scotland should shame us all"', BBC News, 29 June 2021.

147   *'the era of culture wars is over':* Quoted in Peter Walker, 'Era of culture wars is over, pledges new culture secretary Lisa Nandy', *Guardian*, 9 July 2024.

151   *'They deserve better':* @SteveBakerFRSA, Twitter, 27 May 2024.